Innsbruck:
Tramways, trolleybuses and scenic light rail

Ray Deacon

Published by
Light Rail Transit Association
P.O.Box 302
Gloucester GL4 4ZD
ISBN 0-948106-26-3

Contents

This tranquil scene shows car 41 about to pass through the Triumphpforte archway while on a route 3 service to Pradl in ca1929. Left-hand running was still the in force in Innsbruck at that time but the rule was changed to right-hand running in the following April. The Triumphpforte was built following the death of Emperor Franz in 1767 as a memorial from his wife Maria Theresa.

(collection Mackinger)

(FRONT COVER) Built in 1961 for Hagen tramways system and purchased by the AGStb in 1976, car 85 passes through picturesque alpine scenery between Telfeser Wiesen and Luimes, at 1006 metres the highest point on the Stubaitalbahn, in September 1998. Fitted with a centre section from a former Bielefeld car in 1983, it was fully refurbished in 1991 and should remain in service for a further decade.

(Author)

INNSBRUCKER VERKEHRSBETRIEBE

Foreword

The Tram and Trolleybus Services in Innsbruck and the Stubai Valley

Due to the rapid advances in technology in the 19th century and the consequent growth of trade and tourism, it became obvious at an early stage that Tirol, as a transit land, required fast and efficient transport systems for passengers and goods. Already by 1867 Tirol was completely passable from north to south on rail tracks.

This development also roused the requirement for faster and more comfortable transport systems in the city of Innsbruck and it's surrounding region, where the main means of travel was on foot or by horse-drawn vehicles. In 1836 an attempt was made by a businessman to realise a local train service from Innsbruck to Hall, but this failed. The second attempt at a local train service was prepared in 1885. It was sponsored by businessmen, a banker and the railway pioneer Hermann Ritter von Schwind from Augsburg.

The license was granted by the K&K railway ministry in 1889. The local railway train service between Innsbruck and Hall commenced on 1 June 1891 with steam locomotives and rolling stock. This happened without waiting for official permission to open the service, much to the annoyance of the railway authorities, but did not lead to any serious consequences.

On 26 June 1900 the Mittelgebirge railway from Innsbruck to Igls was opened, also powered by steam engines. This railway was built away from the centres of population because of the peoples fears at that time about the new mode of transport and is therefore mainly used for excursions, passing through lovely forest countryside and passed two small lakes to the outskirts of Igls.

On 17 July 1905 the first inner city tram route was opened between the Southern Railway's station (today the main station) and Bergisel, powered by tramcars using direct current. With the extension of this line to Adolf-Pichler-Strasse in the same year (today Conrad Strasse), the regular route of what is today route 1 was completed. Route 3 from Museumstrasse to Lindenstrasse followed in 1911. The tram network was thereby mainly complete, but there were always more extensions and temporary solutions in the tram network.

The satisfactory introduction of electric power in the city area resulted in the conversion to direct current of the local train service between Innsbruck and Hall in 1909/10 and the Mittelgebirge line in 1936.

The tram service today consists of 3 routes. These are route 1 from Bergisel to Hungerburgbahn station over a distance of 4.9 km, route 3 from Amras via the main station to Maria-Theresien Street over a length of 4 km and route 6 (Mittelgebirge train), which in summer runs between the main station and Igls via Bergisel and in winter between Bergisel and Igls. The track length is 11.8 km.

The Stubai Valley Railway:

At the end of the 19th century, the only connection between the Stubai and Wipp valleys and therefore also to Innsbruck was a narrow gravel road. This was no longer acceptable for the increasing tourism and the iron industry of the Stubai valley. A new road planned at that time did not get approval from the municipalities. As an alternative, Hr. Ing. Ritter von Schwind recommended the building of a railway line from Innsbruck via the villages of the Stubai valley through to Matrei in the Wipp valley. Because this long variant appeared too technical and commercially hopeless, another railway pioneer, Hr. Ing. Riehl, was given the contract to plan and establish a shorter route from Innsbruck to Fulpmes

On 17 August 1903 the license for this was granted by the K&K railway ministry. Despite difficult geological conditions, the 18.2 km long route was quickly built using a large workforce. The service was ready for opening on 31 July 1904, using a rare power system of 2500 volt, 42 hz alternating current. In 1983 the power system was changed to 800 volt direct current and re-equipped with vehicles bought from the tram company of the city of Hagen in Germany. Additionally, the route was extended to the main railway station in Innsbruck, increasing the length of the complete route to 21 km. The highest point of the line is near Telfes and is 1006 metres above sea level. The difference in elevation between the highest and lowest points is 413 m and the maximum rate of climb is 50 %.

Trolleybuses:

The decision was made to introduce the trolleybus service in Innsbruck due to the ever increasing scarcity of fuel during World War II, in the hope that the power supply available from the water-powered power stations in it's own region could be maintained. The first trolleybus service was route C from Arzl to Wiltenberg and was opened on 8 April 1944. On 26 June 1944 followed route A from Marktgraben to Hötting and on 9 August 1944 route B from Boznerplatz to Pradl. The trolleybus services were discontinued between 1971 and 1976 due to old age and the last day of service was on route A on 29 February 1976.

Trolleybus routes O and R, using articulated vehicles, were reintroduced in December 1988, because of growing concerns about the ecology and continuous expansion of the housing areas at Olympisches Dorf, Reichenau, and also in the west of the city at Peerhöfe and Höttinger Au. The previous diesel bus routes O and R were discontinued. The trolleybus route O runs on the route Olympisches Dorf - Museumstrasse - St. Georg - Peerhofsiedlung and has a length of 10.5 km. Trolleybus route R runs on the route Reichenau - Hauptbahnhof - Höttinger Au and has a length of 8.4 km.

I am satisfied that our rail and trolleybus system functions well at the moment. Taking into account that our tramcars are already 35 to 40 years old and no longer meet the standards of today in terms of comfort (low-floor technology) and that the maintenance is more and more difficult and expensive, we are currently working with a group of experts, with technical personnel from the city of Innsbruck administration and with the inhabitants to develop a railway concept for Innsbruck, which will also include the Stubaitalbahn. After the concept has been defined, the appropriation of new low-floor cars will be considered. The trolleybuses are also included in these considerations.

Dipl.-Ing. Martin BALTES
Director

Introduction

Development of Innsbruck

The picturesque city of Innsbruck is the capital of the Austrian province of Tirol and is located at the crossroads linking the Trans-European road and rail networks of Germany, Italy and Switzerland. Nestling in a valley 575 metres above sea level, and surrounded by 3300-metre-high mountains, it straddles the fast flowing river Inn. A major cultural and tourist centre, with a thriving trade in timber, crystal, textiles, leather goods and musical instruments, the city has a population of 140 000.

Innsbruck's origins date back to 1180, when a small market settlement was established by Count Berthold of Andechs on land close to the old quarter. A bridge was built across the Inn and this provided the city with its name and insignia. Innsbruck was recognised as an important trading centre as early as the thirteenth century when goods were transported on the river by horse-drawn barges, but only as far as Hall some 8 km downstream, as the river was too treacherous between Hall and Innsbruck.

The city received its charter in 1239, and in 1363 it came under control of the Habsburgs. Archduke Friedrich, also known as the duke of empty pockets, transferred his official residence from Merano in 1420 and declared Innsbruck the capital of Province Tirol. Until quite recently, legend had it that he put an end to jibes about his meanness by building the balcony with a golden roof *(Goldenes Dachl)* when in fact it was built by Maximilian I in 1500. Centuries later, it is a famous landmark and tourist attraction.

After a period of relative tranquillity, the Bavarians tried to invade the province in 1703 during the War of the Spanish Succession, but were repulsed. However, in 1805 Innsbruck was overrun by Napoleon's rampaging army, and three years later came the War of Liberation, the city's most noteworthy contribution to military history. Four fierce battles were fought against the French invaders on a hillside called Berg Isel, during which Andreas Hofer led his Tirolean compatriots to victory and him to national heroism.

The old quarter retains much of its medieval charm and its narrow streets, historic buildings and shopping arcades are a magnet for tourists. Other attractions include the Hofburg Palace, the Wilten Basilica with its beautifully decorated rococo ceiling, abundant museums and two prominent memorials, the *Annasäule* and *Triumphpforte*. Innsbruck was host to the winter Olympics in 1964 and 1976 and the area is a popular holiday destination, offering a wealth of sporting activities throughout the year.

For centuries this mountainous region remained in virtual isolation, the first real opportunity to travel only coming with the advent of the post coach service. Later, Austria became one of the first countries in Europe to build railways; its first line opening between Linz and Budweis in 1827. Its success spawned rapid growth in railway construction across the country and new lines were built throughout the nineteenth and early twentieth centuries. Many were metre-gauge interurban light railways *(Lokalbahnen)*, and three such lines were built in the Innsbruck area: to Hall in 1891, Igls in 1900 and Fulpmes in 1904. They satisfied much of the demand for public transport outside the city, but nothing was provided for people living within until 1905, when the first electric tram route was opened. The system was never large and expanded slowly to a maximum of 6 routes.

To overcome the fuel shortage during the Second World War, when Austria was part of Germany, a three-route trolleybus system was introduced using second-hand vehicles requisitioned by the German authorities from systems in Italy. These were gradually replaced with diesel-engined buses when they became due for replacement and the system slowly contracted until closure in 1976. The damage caused by pollution, however, saw a rapid reversal of policy and the decision to re-introduce trolleybuses was taken a decade later, the first of the second-generation trolleybus routes opening in 1988.

The current tram system comprises two urban routes and two *lokalbahnen*, the latter running high into the mountains to the south of the city. Operated by a fleet of articulated tramcars, the majority obtained second-hand from German systems and restored to pristine condition in the undertaking's workshops, they offer the opportunity to experience the most scenic of rides on tramcars designed for street working.

I first became interested in the Innsbruck tramway system during my first holiday to Austria in 1959, when a day trip to the city was rewarded with the sight of veteran little tramcars crammed full with people. My interest has continued ever since and my intention when writing this book was to convey the fascinating story of the trams and trolleybuses of this fine city, during the centenary year of the opening of the line to Igls.

Acknowledgements

It would have been impossible to produce this book without the invaluable assistance of the following people, to whom I offer my sincere thanks:

Hr. Martin Baltes, Hr. Oskar Schreiber and **Fr. Beate Blechinger** of **Innsbrucker Verkehrsbetriebe**, for information on current operations and plans for future developments.

Hr. Dieter Seifridsberger and **Hr. Walter Kreutz** (TMB), for information on the preservation scene, museum society activities, the loan of historical photographs, and factual verification of the text.

Hr. Gunter Mackinger (Salzburger Lokalbahn), for the loan of photographs from his collection.

Roger Smith, for producing yet another excellent series of high quality maps.

Michael Taplin, Michael Lea and **Roger Jones** of the LRTA.

Janet Taplin (Just my Type), for typesetting the draft text and the final design of the page layout.

Michael Russell and **Alan Murray**, for verification of the trolleybus chapter and tables, and the loan of colour slides.

And lastly, but by no means least, the late **Jack Wyse** (LRTA), for his advice on the textual content and for proof reading the initial draft. As a tribute to him, the technical summaries he submitted describing ac and dc traction supplies and the control system of car 60 are included.

To all others whose names are accredited with having taken specific photographs.

A special thank you to my wife **Rosemary** and son **Kees** for their support and company on our trips to the Innsbruck area.

Ray Deacon, Blackboys, East Sussex. April 2000.

1. The undertakings

Shortly after the turn of the century, three *Lokalbahnen* were being operated out of Innsbruck under the management of separate companies. This chapter describes their gestation and early years of operation.

The port of Hall

Until the early nineteenth century, public transport in the Innsbruck area was virtually non-existent and only the more affluent could afford horse-drawn carriages or the postcoach fare. Roads were no more than bumpy rutted tracks and very uncomfortable to travel on, even in those carriages fitted with superior suspension.

The village of Hall was a thriving riverside port on the north bank of the river Inn, some 8 kilometres (km) downstream of Innsbruck. As the river between the two localities was too shallow for the movement of barges, goods bound for Innsbruck from the east of the country were unloaded onto horse-drawn wagons at Hall; a laborious and time consuming task.

In 1887, August Riedinger and Louis Hirsch, two merchants from Augsburg, Anton Prantl, the Innkeeper at Gasthaus Dollinger in Mühlau, and Hermann Ritter von Schwind, an experienced railway engineer, published a proposal for a narrow gauge *Lokalbahn* between Hall and Innsbruck, with a rural section operated under steam power and an urban section as a conventional horse-drawn tramway. The change of motive power was considered essential if opposition to pollution from the locomotives was to be placated. The passenger vehicles would be built of lightweight materials to facilitate operation by both forms of propulsion. Later the following year, the proposal was revised to allow operation of the complete line with steam-powered locomotives; a public relations exercise having reduced the anti-steam faction to an ineffective minority.

A concession to build the line was granted on 18 September 1889, on condition that construction began immediately and was completed within 2 years so as to keep disruption to a minimum. Track laying was soon underway and drawings prepared for the locomotives, passenger vehicles and goods trailers.

From a terminus at Unteren Stadtplatz in Hall, the 11-km long route would follow the northern bank of the river Inn, skirting the villages of Thaur, Rum and Arzl to Mühlau, from where it would cross the river on a purpose-built bridge (the Kettenbrücke), and continue via Falkstrasse and Herzog-Otto-Strasse to Maria-Theresien-Strasse. The final section would take it via Salurner Strasse to Südbahnhof - the main station which took its name from the Südbahn railway and was renamed Hauptbahnhof in 1919. The metre-gauge line would comprise long sections of single-track and passing loops with a maximum speed limited of 10 km/h within built-up areas and 25 km/h on the country sections.

As no suitable site could be found for a depot in the central area, a plot of land was purchased at Berg Isel on the southern outskirts of the city, and the decision taken to divert the route via Triumphpforte, Leopoldstrasse and Wiltener Platz to Berg Isel, increasing its length to 12.14 km.

Four 0-4-0 steam locomotives (numbered 1-4) were ordered from Krauss of Linz, and *Lok* 1 arrived in the summer of 1890. It was soon making test runs on the rural section between Mühlau and Rum, where speeds of 40 km/h were achieved. The order for 14 passenger trailers and one goods wagon was placed with Weitzer of Graz. Progress continued at a steady pace and Berg Isel depot was ready for use by the end of the year with track laying completed by April 1891.

The passenger cars were built to the standard horse-tram design of the period, with four-bay wooden bodies, open platforms and 2-axle trucks. An attractive dark green livery, highlighted with the provincial coat-of-arms, provided a handsome passenger vehicle. Accommodation was provided for 14 passengers on wooden bench-style seating in the saloon, and a further 2 on each platform. Standing room was available for 6 passengers inside and 7 on each platform, making a total capacity of 38. They were given fleet numbers 1-14 and several were to run in regular passenger service into the 1980s.

An LBIHiT train leaves a trail of smoke as it exits from Maria-Theresien-Strasse and is about to pass through the Triumphpforte into Leopoldstrasse while en-route from Hall to Berg Isel in 1895. (W.Kreutz)

The first passenger trains began operating on 1 June 1891 on an hourly headway, and remarkably few problems were encountered during the first few weeks. As passenger loadings rapidly increased and trains were often filled to capacity, two more locomotives (*Loks 5* and *6*) were ordered from Krauss and four more passenger cars (15-18) from Graz in 1892 to enable the headway to be reduced to half-hourly. This batch of cars had open-sided saloons fitted with roll-down awnings for protection during inclement weather and proved very popular during the summer months. A follow-on order for five more enclosed-saloon, open-platform passenger cars (19-23) and another goods wagon was supplied by Graz in 1893.

Lokalbahn Innsbruck-Hall in Tirol (LBIHiT)

On 17 June 1893, the railway gained its legal credentials when it was officially named "Lokalbahn Innsbruck-Hall in Tirol" (**LBIHiT**). The locals had their own affectionate interpretation "**L**angsam **b**in **i**ch **h**alt **i**m **t**empo", which loosely translates to "I am slow but I can't help it".

All rolling stock was housed at Berg Isel, but following the construction of a small depot at the Hall terminus in 1895, two locomotives and six trailers were stabled overnight in the new shed.

Four years later, a short-working was introduced from Berg Isel to Mühlau (Gasthaus Dollinger) running on a 30-minute headway. As this supplemented the existing 30-minute service to Hall, a train ran every 15 minutes on the section between Berg Isel and Mühlau. To operate this service, two larger locomotives (7 and 8) were ordered from Krauss, and six more open-platform passenger cars (24-29) from Graz for delivery in 1900.

Apart from the line to Hall, Innsbruck was without any form of public transport as the new century dawned. In response to growing public demand, the LBIHiT published a proposal for a tram route running from Claudiaplatz in the northern suburb of Saggen to Wilten Bahnhof (renamed Westbahnhof in 1919) in the south-west. The rolling stock would comprise horse-drawn tramcars similar to those operating on the Hall line. The Council, however, rejected the proposal as it preferred an electrically-propelled system, and the city's first power station was still under construction.

In this early view a train, comprising a rake of three cars in the immaculate LBIHiT dark green livery, preparing to depart Berg Isel for a run to Hall. Of interest is the open Summer car in the centre with sunshades already in place. (F.Fritz)

At the other end of the line, the Hall terminus was located in a square called Unteren Stadtplatz. In this 1905 view, the locomotive is seen shunting a goods wagon round the carriages prior to returning to Innsbruck. (W.Kreutz)

6

The Mittelgebirge plateau

The Mittelgebirge plateau and its scattering of small communities lies south-east of and 300 metres above Innsbruck. Towards the latter part of the nineteenth century these communities had begun to expand and, as they were cut off for much of the winter their appointed committees approached the City Council for authorisation to construct a railway link into the city.

On 26 February 1896, the Council appointed a Swiss company, Maschinenfabrik Oerlikon (MFO), as concessionaire for the construction of a steam-powered *Lokalbahn* between Berg Isel and Igls, serving the villages of Ambras, Aldrans and Lans, and construction of the first 3.6-kilometre section to Ambras began in August 1899. Two 0-6-2 locomotives were purchased from Krauss, and twelve LBIHiT-type 2-axle passenger cars with open platforms, two enclosed and two open goods wagons from Graz in 1900. Because of the extremely tight curves encountered on the line, the engine coal bunker was mounted on a single axle and attached to the main body of the engine by an articulated joint. A depot was erected on the existing Berg Isel site to house the rolling stock.

Innsbrucker Mittelgebirgsbahn (IMB)

The LBIHiT was given responsibility for the administration of the line, but the City Council insisted that a separate company, the *Innsbrucker Mittelgebirgsbahn* (IMB), managed the operational requirements. The locomotives were numbered 1 and 2, the passenger cars 101-12, the covered goods wagons 113-4 and the open goods wagons 115-6.

The line was opened on 27 June 1900, when a special train, comprising *Lok* 2 and trailer cars 101/6/10, carried invited guests and members of the press to Igls and back. On arrival back at Berg Isel the rear trailer derailed, causing an embarrassed party to transfer to another train to complete the journey to the Rathaus.

Public service began on the following day on an hourly-schedule between 06:00 and 21:00 on weekdays, and until 13:30 on Sundays and holidays. The afternoon service on these days ran half-hourly to cater for the large number of excursionists and walkers, but it soon became apparent that there was not enough turn-round time for engine coal bunkers to be replenished and the headways were extended to 40 minutes. Shortly before the line had opened, the LBIHiT advised the IMB that four locomotives would be required to run the proposed timetable, but the IMB ignored this on the grounds of cost. As a consequence, chaotic scrambles occurred whenever trains were turned-round on busy days. The IMB was thus forced to purchase a third locomotive and *Lok* 3 was delivered by Krauss on 12 April 1901.

Because of the steep gradients encountered, trains bound for Igls were limited to six trailers, but an extra two were added if required for the return journey; spare trailers being hauled up to Igls during less busy times of the day. A run up to Igls took 24 minutes with 26 minutes scheduled for the return trip.

The line was well patronised and the number of passengers carried in 1902 saw an increase of 30% over the previous year. A common complaint, however,

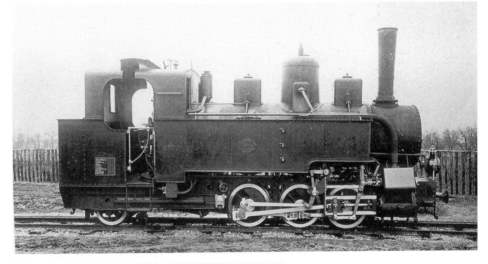

This official photograph is of one of the locomotives built for service on the IMB and was taken in 1900 at the Krauss works, Linz. The unusual articulation for the bunker is clearly visible.   (F.Fritz)

The Lanser See halt on the Mittelgebirgsbahn in 1910 sees passengers alighting from an Igls bound train to take in the fresh mountain air.   (W.Kreutz)

(above) Igls station ca1912 with a train having just arrived from Innsbruck. Apart from the station buildings, the Mittelgebirge plateau has changed substantially in the intervening years. Two of the carriages waiting on the stub-end track nearest the camera are waiting to be coupled to the next busy down-train. (below) Another view of the same location, shows the canvas screens that were fitted to the car platforms facing the locomotive for the uphill run.
(J.O. Slezak)

was that passengers using the open platforms of the trailers on heavily laden trains were showered with soot and sparks. The problem was resolved by fitting canvas screens to the platforms, and the platform nearest the engine was reserved for the carriage of mail.

The Stubai valley

The serene and picturesque Stubaital with its delightful villages of Mieders, Telfes, Fulpmes and Neustift diverges off the Brenner Pass at Schönberg some 10 km south of Innsbruck, and an abundance of leisure activities attract thousands of tourists into the valley throughout the year.

It was, however, the increasing production from the iron, silver and lead mines at Fulpmes that first brought about the demand for direct links to Innsbruck. As late

as 1895, workers were still being brought in from nearby hamlets by horse-drawn carts, and a more efficient means of transporting them, and shipping the raw materials to a convenient railhead, was eagerly sought.

The LBIHiT director Ing. Ritter von Schwind, fresh from his success with the construction of the Hall line, proposed that a railway should be built from Berg Isel to Stefansbrücke and up the north side of the Stubai valley to Telfes. From there it would run down to Fulpmes, across the valley to Mieders, and on through Schönberg to re-enter the Brenner Pass and terminus at Matrei; a distance of 38 km. His proposal was approved at a villages' committee meeting on 22 July 1895, but as construction was about to begin the Südbahn (mainline railway) announced its intention to build a station at

Matrei on its line running through the Brenner Pass to Italy. Even though this would have had no significant impact on the proposed Stubaital line, the committee could not agree on the viability of the section from Fulpmes to Matrei and the whole project was shelved.

Two years later, Ing. von Schwind and two colleagues, Ing. Miller and Ing. Riehl, published an alternative proposal for a rail line into the Stubaital over a different route. Starting at Wiltener Pfarrkirche, close to Berg Isel, it would follow a route via Natters, Mutters and Telfes to Fulpmes. Options included an extension to Neustift and a branch linking Fulpmes to Matrei via Mieders and Schönberg. Approval to proceed with the Innsbruck to Fulpmes section was agreed at the next committee meeting, and a piece of land to the south of Wiltener Pfarrkirche was purchased for the depot and terminus. Operation would be by steam-hauled trains comprising passenger cars similar to those of the IMB, running on metre-gauge tracks. Ing. Riehl was appointed construction manager and he was soon at work preparing the tender documentation.

Alternating current traction

At the turn of the century, electric traction was normally by direct current (dc) supply, but this was generally limited by the available insulation to a maximum of 1000 volts, with a single contact wire or rail. Some French installations managed to "cheat" by the Sécheron system which had a contact wire at, for example, +1000 volts plus a third rail at -1000 V, and designing the installation so that the insulation did not have to exceed 1000 volts as the body potential was nominally 0 volts. Relatively later, feasible dc contact-wire voltages rose to about 3 kV.

It is less well known that the rather small number of higher-voltage alternating-current traction supplies were polyphase, normally three-phase with two overhead contact wires plus running rails. This required a three-phase installation to be "unbalanced" in the sense that, instead of a "neutral" earth, one of the three phases was earthed, and complications of dual overhead collection ensured that junctions were intricate with lots of inelegant metal and insulator in the sky.

What then of single-phase alternating current traction? The simple answer is that it was not used because no motor was available until 1902-3 when Winter and Eichberg designed the first single-phase traction motor for AEG-Union. Because it was a rather crude design and tended to arc and burn at the commutator, AEG was obliged to subsidise early trials on a running installation.

Stubaitalbahn(Stb)

The AEG-Union company submitted a bid to build the line and equip it with their unproven electrical system based on single contact wire supplying ac at 2.5 kV and a frequency of 42.5 Hz. AEG demonstrated its confidence in the system by purchasing shares in the operating company, and supplied three motor cars at no cost. The passenger trailers and goods wagons would be purchased by the operating company. The bid was eagerly accepted and an order placed with Graz for the following rolling stock:

* Three motor cars (1-3) — 11.4 metres long and 2.4 metres wide, with an unladen weight of 20.5 tonnes and capacity for 32 seated and 33 standing passengers. Fully-enclosed saloons with two compartments separated by a high-voltage electrical equipment section, and another section for mail and small packages. The smaller 2nd class compartment provided accommodation for eight passengers and the larger 3rd class compartment could seat twenty-four. Windscreens were provided for driver protection. The all-wood body was mounted on two American-design equal-wheeled bogies, each fitted with a single

Two motor cars cross the Mutterer Brücke on the Stubaitalbahn during a test run prior to the line's opening in 1904. To the right is the 250-metre-long tunnel leading north to Nockhofweg.
(W.Kreutz)

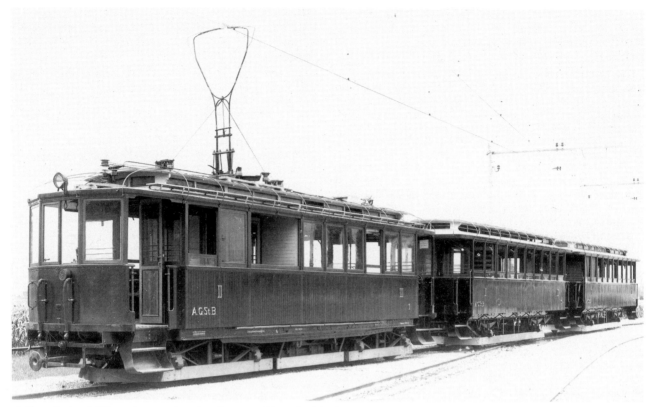

A fine study of Stb motor car 1 and trailer cars 11 and 16 in the all-over brown livery outside Stubaitalbahnhof before the start of operations in 1904.
(collection Mackinger)

Winter Eichberg WE-31 motor rated at 30-kW. Two bow collectors were mounted on a clerestory style roof; one for the 2.5 kV ac supply on the interurban section, and the other for use under the proposed 600-volt ac supply of the city tramway. This was subsequently installed with a dc supply.

* Six trailers (11-16) — 10 metres long and 2.4 metres wide, with an unladen weight of 7.0 tonnes and capacity for 38 seated and 22 standing passengers. Constructed of wood, the fully-enclosed saloon had a single 3rd-class compartment and open platforms, and was mounted on a 2-axle truck with 4-metre wheelbase.

Construction of the steeply-graded 18.16-km adhesion line, which began on 1 May 1903, required the employment of over 800 men and took thirteen months to complete. Quite an achievement considering that the track was laid on private right-of-way throughout, and

required several major obstacles to be overcome along the way. The most prominent of these were two tunnels of 150 and 220 metres in length which had to be bored through solid rock, and two 109-metre long, 25-metre high, steel girder bridges. Because of the numerous curves encountered along the route, the maximum operating speed was limited to 25 km/h.

Stations and halts were constructed at Berg Isel, Plateau, Gärberbach, Natters, Mutters (passing loop), Raitis, Kreith (passing loop), Luimes-Mieders, Telfes (passing loop) and Fulpmes.

Aktiengesellschaft Stubaitalbahn (AGStb)

The operating company Aktiengesellschaft Stubaitalbahn was formed on 8 November 1903. Its first motor car, numbered 1 and sporting an all-brown livery, arrived on 7 July 1904 and was followed within weeks by motor cars 2 and 3, passenger trailer cars 11-16 and

Stb motor car 1 again, this time coupled to open wagon 22 and covered wagon 31 shortly before the opening of the line. The carriage of goods provided valuable additional income for the AGStb until the conversion to dc operation in 1983.
(collection Mackinger)

Another photograph of Stb motor car 1 on test, sees it running down past Wilten Bahnhof with engineers and company staff on board. *(W.Kreutz)*

31 July, 1904, and the official opening ceremony of the Stubaitalbahn is underway at Fulpmes, the local dignitaries and invited guests having ridden the 18 km from Innsbruck in the two decorated motor cars. *(W.Kreutz)*

goods wagons 21-22 and 31-32. Unfortunately, the first test run which took place on 27 July, using cars 3 and 13, came to a premature halt when a large drop in voltage stranded the train some 400 metres up the mountainside. As the motor cars were able to operate solo at this lower voltage, the decision was taken to begin operations with a skeleton service without the trailers.

The official opening took place on 31 July 1904 when two decorated motor cars, filled with local dignitaries, made inaugural runs from Berg Isel to Fulpmes. Stations along the line were adorned with bunting, fires were lit on the mountain tops and torchlight processions held in the evening. For this was a long awaited and momentous occasion, and one which the population determined to celebrate in their traditional manner. As the AGStb had no experience of running a railway, operational control was undertaken by the LBIHiT. It produced a provisional timetable which came into effect on the following day.

By the end of the year so many passengers were using the line that a fourth motor car had to be purchased. Delivered by Graz in April 1905, car 4 had longer platforms than the earlier batch and sported a revised livery of brown with cream window frames. The windows in the 2nd class compartment were elongated to provide passengers, willing to pay a premium fare, with uninterrupted views of the Alpine scenery.

The number of passengers carried on the Stubaitalbahn (Stb) continued to exceed expectations, but it was the high volume of goods that caught the AGStb unawares. To cater for this lucrative trade, two more open (Gw 23-4) and two enclosed (Gw 33-4) goods wagons were purchased from Graz in 1905.

Two views of Stb motor car 4, (left) crossing the Mutterer Brücke en-route to Innsbruck (collection Mackinger) and (below), with crew and passengers posing for the camera alongside the Sonnenburgerhof hotel during its construction. The extra length of this car compared to cars 1-3 enabled small upright windows to be fitted to the platform sides and large "panoramic" windows were installed in the 2nd class compartment. The cream-painted upper half easily distinguished this car from the other three for many years. (H. Herrmann)

2. Urban tramways

In May 1904, the Council authorised the LBIHiT to construct an electrically operated urban tramway running from Claudiaplatz in the northern suburb of Saggen to Wilten station in the south, and from there into Egger-Lienz-Strasse and over the Arlberg railway on a tram-only viaduct to the Berg Isel terminus shared by the Hall and Igls steam lines. As the Stubaitalbahn line to Fulpmes also terminated nearby, it was a logical decision to build the new tramway to the same focal point.

Seven 2-axle double-ended motor cars, numbered 36-42, were delivered by Waggonfabrik Graz for the new service. Powered by 2 x 21.7-kW motors, they provided accommodation for 16 seated passengers on wooden longitudinal benches in a four-bay saloon and 16 standing passengers, some inside the saloon, and the remainder on the rear platform. Glazed windscreens were fitted from the outset.

located, to Berg Isel was opened first and all seven trams were needed to run a 7½-minute headway on weekdays, 15 minutes on Sundays. The fares were set at 16 Heller from Süd Tiroler Platz to Wilten station and 20 Heller for the full journey to Berg Isel (from 1900 to 1925 the currency was 1 Krone = 100 Heller).

Construction of the 1.6-km section from Museumstrasse to Claudiaplatz via Ing.-Etzel-Strasse then commenced, using grooved rail throughout. Three more motor cars (43-5) were ordered from Graz to provide the rolling stock for the extended route, which was opened for passenger service on 10 November 1905. A final extension via a one-way loop to the lower terminus of the Hungerburgbahn cable railway was added in 1924.

New trailers and a second tram route

Also in 1906, a further two motor cars (46-7) and four 2-axle passenger trailers (61-4) were ordered from Graz to alleviate overcrowding, and some of the Hall trailers

Another view of a car on test, this time of red and white liveried LBIHiT motor car 41, seen crossing the Arlbergbahn on the tram-only viaduct shortly before the opening of the urban system in 1905. (W.Kreutz)

The permanent way equipment was supplied by the AEG/Union company which subcontracted the construction of the single-track line to a company called Riehl. Built to metre-gauge standards and with passing loops at strategic locations, the track used grooved rail in streets not shared with the Hall steam trams. Power was fed from the overhead wire at 550 volts dc (later 600 volts) via a bow collector.

The initial police inspection took place in early July 1905 using motor car 40 and goods wagon 32, both cars laden with sandbags to simulate passenger loadings, followed by a second inspection using motor car 41 and three trailers on 14 July. Speed limits of 6 km/h were imposed in the narrow Burggraben; 8 km/h on the viaduct over the Arlbergbahn and 12 km/h elsewhere. Conductors were instructed to alight at Burggraben and Berg Isel depot yard and walk in front of their trams to ensure the safety of pedestrians.

On 15 July 1905, to much jubilation, decorated cars 40 and 42 made their inaugural runs carrying invited guests and local dignitaries. When the speeches were finished, the other five cars entered service, their bright red and white livery contrasting well with the grey of the city and snow-capped mountains beyond. The section from Süd Tiroler Platz, where the main station was

were adapted for working with the motor cars. Delivery of the new trailers began in June, but it was November before the motor cars arrived. The bodies on the trailers were identical to those on the motor cars except for longer open platforms.

With sufficient rolling stock for its immediate needs, the LBIHiT focused its attention on building more routes and electrifying the line to Hall. Construction of a second tram route from Süd Tiroler Platz, running via Salurner Strasse, Triumphpforte and Maximilianstrasse, to the junction at Andreas-Hofer-Strasse was soon under way, and this was opened on the 13 June 1908. Extra capacity for the route was provided by modifying more steam trailers.

The installation of more passenger stops on the *Stubaitalbahn* encouraged the construction of several hotels along the route. One of these, the Sonnenburgerhof, was built on the hillside overlooking Innsbruck, close to the halt called Plateau. As it was the only landmark of note in the vicinity, the halt was renamed Sonnenburgerhof in 1907. A year later, a new halt was built at Nockhofweg, above Mutters, to cater for the influx of skiers using the expanding facilities on the Nockspitze mountain.

(above) The location for this opening day scene is Andreas-Hofer-Strasse and one of the decorated ceremonial cars (40 or 42) is captured passing service car 38 on this long-awaited occasion, 15 July, 1905. (W.Kreutz) The Triumphpforte and Maximilianstrasse provide the setting (below) for LBIHiT motor car 35 as it waits at the stop. (collection Mackinger)

Electrifying the Hall line

Contracts for the electrification of the Hall line were awarded to AEG which began work on the conversion in the spring of 1908. The opportunity was also taken to divert the tracks from Falkstrasse over a parallel route via Kaiserjägerstrasse. Eight, fully enclosed, equal-wheeled bogie tramcars were ordered from Graz/AEG, with seating for 30 people on two-and-one seats and space for 20 standing passengers. An additional four passengers could stand on the rear platform and four more were allowed at the front with the driver.

Power was fed at 550 volts dc on the urban section and on the country section beyond Mühlau, at 1000 volts dc (later 1200 volts) for which a second bow was fitted. Equipped with 2 x 36.8-kW motors these cars were powerful enough to haul four fully-laden trailers along the relatively flat course of the line, and at higher average speeds than the steam trains. As events transpired, only four tram-sets were required to operate the 30-minute headway.

The complete batch of cars arrived in the summer of 1909, painted in the red and white livery and numbered 1-8. During the year, the remaining unmodified LBIHiT-owned steam trailers were equipped with electric lighting and heating in the Berg Isel workshops. Following successful test running and conversion training for drivers, electric services were introduced on the section from Berg Isel to Landeshauptschiessstand near Mühlau, on the 28 August 1909. The country section to Hall continued to be operated by steam, until electric traction took over on 7 January 1910.

Numbered 32-35 these cars arrived during the summer of 1911 and route 3 was extended to Pradl on 30 December.

Integrating the fleets

As the trailers used by both the IMB and the LBIHiT were identical, (except that the IMB cars were fitted with both air and solenoid braking from new whereas the braking on the LBIHiT cars was not brought up to this standard until later) and were housed and maintained in Berg Isel depot, the companies agreed to combine them in a single series and renumber the Hall cars. At that time, the IMB cars were numbered 101-12 and the LBIHiT cars from 1-29. In 1910/11, the LBIHiT cars were renumbered 113-41 and cars 61-64 became 142-5. The open goods wagons were numbered from 201 and the enclosed wagons from 251. The structure of the passenger fleets in 1913 was as follows:

6 January, 1910, the last day of steam operation on the LBIHiT. The proud crew pose in front of their diminutive steed before departing Berg Isel for Mühlau.
(collection Mackinger)

More cars and route numbering

Work had also begun laying tracks for a tram route from Andreas-Hofer-Strasse to Mühlau, running via Fischergasse, Wiltener Platz, Leopoldstrasse, Triumphpforte, Maria-Theresien-Strasse, Marktgraben, Herzog-Otto-Strasse, Rennweg, Kaiserjägerstrasse and Hungerburgbahn, and another seven 2-axle motor cars (48-54) were ordered from Graz to provide the rolling stock. Coincident with its opening on 5 November 1909, the following route numbering system came into use:

1: **Berg Isel** — Maria-Theresien-Str. — **Hungerburgbahn**

2: **Andreas-Hofer-Str.** — Fischerstr. — Wiltener Platz — Maria-Theresien-Str. — Marktgraben — Rennweg — Hungerburgbahn — **Mühlau**

3: **Andreas-Hofer-Str**. — Maximilianstr. — Süd Tiroler Platz — Brunecker Str. — **Museumstr.**

4: **Berg Isel** — Maria-Theresien-Str. — Rennweg — Hungerburgbahn — Mühlau — **Landeshauptschiessstand** (to Hall from January 1910)

The LBIHiT, continuing with its expansionist policies made a bid to take over and electrify the Innsbrucker Mittelgebirgsbahn, using the spare Hall bogie cars, but it was unsuccessful on this occasion. Undaunted, it applied instead for a concession to extend route 3 from Museumstrasse to Lindengasse in Pradl. The concession was granted and four more 2-axle motor cars were ordered from Graz to operate the extended route.

LBIHiT

Fleet No.	Built by	Year built	Type	Original No.
Motor cars				
1-8	Graz	1909	4xZR	
32-35	Graz	1911	2xZR	
36-45	Graz	1905	2xZR	
46-47	Graz	1908	2xZR	
48-54	Graz	1909	2xZR	
Trailer cars				
113-126	Graz	1891	2xZR	1-14
127-130	Graz	1892	2xZR	15-18
131-135	Graz	1893	2xZR	19-23
136-141	Graz	1900	2xZR	24-29
142-145	Graz	1908	2xZR	61-64

IMB

	Built by	Year built	Type	
Trailer cars				
101-112	Graz	1900	2xZR	

Stubaitalbahn

	Built by	Year built	Type	
Motor cars				
1-3	Graz	1904	4xZR	
4	Graz	1905	4xZR	
Trailer cars				
11-16	Graz	1904	2xZR	

The activities that seem to be interesting the public in this ca1907 photograph of Maria-Theresien-Strasse, are due to the appearance of a Stubaitalbahn trailer in the city centre. It is possibly being hauled by a LBIHiT motor car during tests to assess if services on the Stb could be extended into the centre. (J.O.Slezak)

Trailer 144 was one of a batch of four Graz-built cars delivered in 1906 to bolster passenger capacity on LBIHiT services. It is shown here at Berg Isel depot in near original condition, including matchwood lower side panels. (ETB)

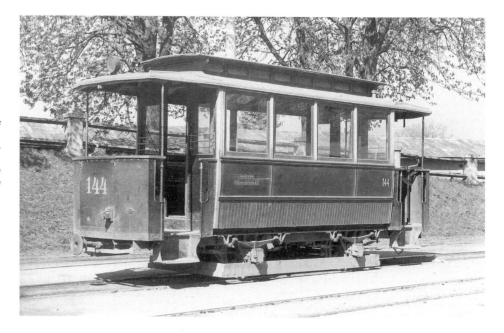

It is late 1909 and a recently delivered Hall bogie car hauls a rake of steam-hauled stock on a test run along the line to Hall. It is seen on the passing loop at Thaur a few weeks before the conversion to electric operation. Both bow collectors drew power when operating under 1000v dc on the country section. (W.Kreutz)

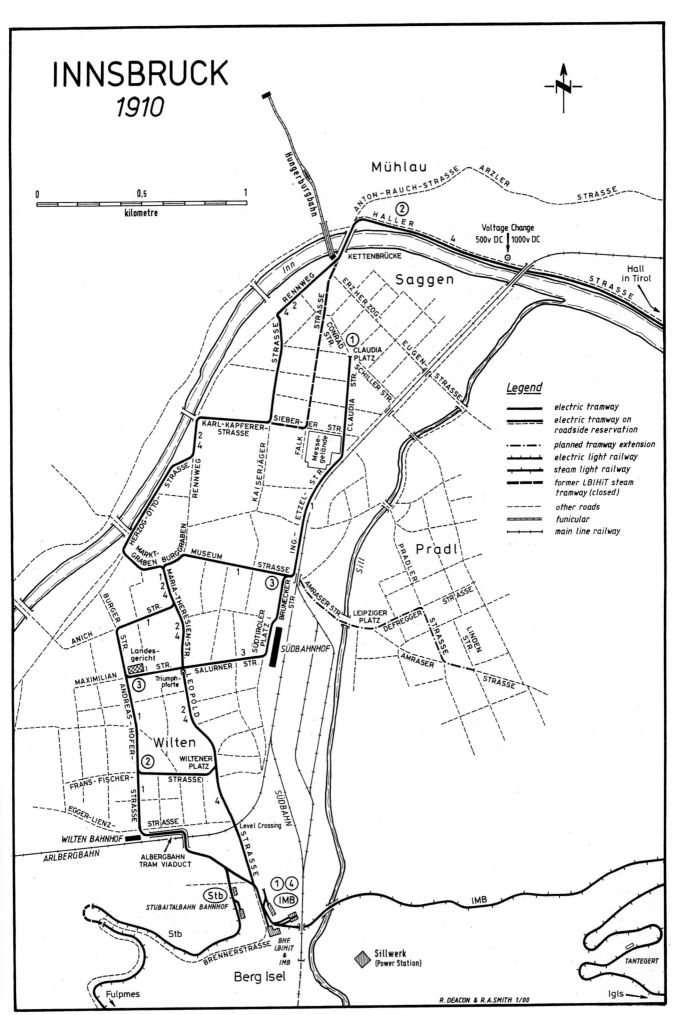

INNSBRUCK
1910

0   0,5   1
kilometre

N

Mühlau

ANTON-RAUCH-STRASSE   ARZLER   STRASSE

Hungerburgbahn

HALLER

Inn

RENNWEG

KETTENBRÜCKE

Saggen

ERZ-HERZOG-

CONRAD STR.

STRASSE

STRASSE

CLAUDIA PLATZ

SCHILLER STR.

EUGEN-STRASSE

Voltage Change
500v DC ↓ 1000v DC

Hall in Tirol
STRASSE

KARL-KAPFERER-STRASSE

SIEBER-ER STR.

KAISERJÄGER

FALK

Messe-gelände

CLAUDIA STR.

ING.-ETZEL-STR.

HERZOG-OTTO-STRASSE

RENNWEG

BURGER

ANICH

MARKT-GRABEN   BURGGRABEN   MUSEUM   STRASSE

Sill

Pradl

PRADLER STRASSE

STRASSE

LINDEN STR.

BRUNECKER STR.

AMRASER STR.

LEIPZIGER PLATZ

DEFREGGER STRASSE

AMRASER   STRASSE

MAXIMILIAN

Landes-gericht

STR.

MARIA-THERESIEN-STR.

SÜDTIROLER PLATZ

SÜDBAHNHOF

Triumph-pforte

SALURNER   STR.

LEOPOLD

ANDREAS-HOFER-STRASSE

Wilten

WILTENER PLATZ

FRANS-FISCHER-STRASSE

EGGER-LIENZ-STRASSE   STRASSE

SÜDBAHN

STRASSE

Level Crossing

WILTEN BAHNHOF
ARLBERGBAHN

ALBERGBAHN TRAM VIADUCT

STUBAITALBAHN BAHNHOF

Stb

BRENNERSTRASSE

BHF. LBIHiT & IMB

Berg Isel

Fulpmes

Stb   IMB

IMB

Sillwerk
(Power Station)

TANTEGERT

Igls →

R. DEACON & R.A.SMITH 1/00

Legend

— electric tramway
═ electric tramway on roadside reservation
—·— planned tramway extension
━ electric light railway
▬ steam light railway
—— former LBIHiT steam tramway (closed)
- - - other roads
═ funicular
┼┼┼ main line railway

Cars 54 and 47 pass in Leopoldstrasse while operating on route 2. The Triumphpforte can be seen in the distance and the snow-capped Nordkette mountain range completes the setting. Route 2 was closed in 1926 but Leopoldstrasse continued to be used by trams until the mid-1960s.
(collection Mackinger)

The steam stock comprised the following locomotives:

LBIHIT

Fleet No.	Built by	Year built	Type
1-2	Krauss	1890	0-4-0T
3-6	Krauss	1891	0-4-0T
7-8	Krauss	1900	0-4-0T

IMB

Fleet No.	Built by	Year built	Type
1-2	Krauss	1900	0-6-2T
3	Krauss	1901	0-6-2T

The number of cars required to operate the services increased with each extension, or when headways were reduced. In 1913 for example, seven 2-axle motor/trailer sets were rostered for route 1, five sets for route 2, four solo motor cars for route 3 and four bogie cars with up to four trailers each on route 4. Tram sets on route 1 often comprised a motor car with one of the large trailer cars (142-5) and one former steam trailer, as this was the busiest urban route.

Early in 1914, a proposal was published for the construction of the Sellrain Valley Railway *(Sellraintalbahn)*. Sharing the Stb tracks from Berg Isel it would branch off at Natters, and head in a westerly direction through the villages of Götzens, Axams and Grinzens to Gries in Sellrain, some 1210 metres above sea level. Unfortunately, the onset of war curtailed its progression, and subsequent attempts to revive it were unsuccessful.

Although taken shortly before the Second World War, this view of car 35 at the route 3 terminus at Lindengasse, Pradl, shows how little the area had changed in the years since the route's opening.
(W.Kreutz)

3. World war 1 and the early 'twenties

With the outbreak of war on 1 August 1914 came the mobilisation of troops and reservists; many of whom worked for the tramway companies. By the early months of 1915, crew shortages had become so acute that women were taken on to work as conductresses. They were issued with black uniforms, similar to those of the men, and all crews were issued with yellow arm bands to distinguish them from the militia. As the postcoach services to Hall also suffered manpower shortages, the carriage of the mails was transferred to the trams.

In 1916, passenger loadings rose sharply prompting the introduction of longer tram-sets on each of the urban routes. The 2-axle motor cars were permanently coupled with a trailer, and a second trailer was added when available, while the bogie cars ran with four trailers on all route 4 duties. Spare Hall bogie cars were allocated to route 2 to increase capacity on this busy route, and a reversing triangle was installed at the Pradl terminus of route 3 to provide a means for the motor cars to run-round their trailers.

Ambulance trams

As the war drew on, additional responsibilities were placed on the tramcars. The most demanding of these was the transfer of wounded soldiers from ambulance trains from the main station and Westbahnhof to hospitals in Innsbruck, Hall and via the Stubaitalbahn line to Fulpmes. Army engineers installed extra tram tracks at both main stations to provide easier access for these hospital specials, and a branch from Lindengasse on route 3 into the Conradkaserne (military barracks) which had been converted to an emergency hospital.

Goods wagon 253 was adapted to carry stretchers, and two 1907-built fully enclosed trailers were

(left) Several tramcars were adapted for ambulance duties during the First World War to transport wounded soldiers to hospitals in the city. In this photograph, taken in 1916, a casualty is loaded into a goods wagon outside Südbahnhof. (below) Trailer car 147 was one of a pair purchased from Merano in 1917 and used initially on ambulance duties. During rebuilding in 1947 the clerestory roof was removed and the car is seen in this condition at Berg Isel with motor car 44 and two Hall trailers. (W.Kreutz)

Circular route 0 operated from June to August 1923 only, so photographs of cars on it are rare. In this scenic view looking north along Maria-Theresien-Strasse, motor car 36 has just turned from Anichstrasse. The tall column is the Annasäule, erected to commemorate victory over the Bavarians in the War of the Spanish Succession, 1703. (W.Kreutz)

purchased from Merano (ex-53-4) and similarly converted. They were initially given fleet numbers 1B-2B, but were renumbered 146-7 in the passenger fleet following the cessation of hostilities. Trailer cars 127-8/31/3 and goods wagons 203-4 comprised the remaining ambulance cars, with both 2- and 4-axle motor cars providing the motive power.

As the First World War progressed, and the number of casualties overwhelmed the hospitals in the city, many hotels on the *Mittelgebirge* were prepared for use as temporary hospitals. As there were no motor vehicles to transfer the wounded by road they were transferred by the IMB. A special train set was formed, comprising a number of goods wagons and passenger trailer 109, and the first casualties were transferred from military hospitals to Igls in early 1916. Hall bogie cars hauled the trains as far as Berg Isel from where IMB steam locomotives took over.

When Italy joined the conflict on the Anglo-French side in 1915, a rehabilitation centre was built in the Stubai valley at Mieders and a military hospital and army barracks in Fulpmes, causing a significant increase in the volume of traffic using the *Stubaitalbahn*. Seriously wounded soldiers were transferred to hospitals in the Stubaital, while those able to return to battle were taken down to Innsbruck on trains commandeered by the military as and when required.

Another major task was the carriage of potatoes, vegetables and milk brought down from the mountain pastures, bordering the IMB and Stb lines, to distribution centres in the city and villages along the line to Hall.

All this activity increased the wear on motors and controllers, at a time when parts and materials were difficult to obtain. The skills of the workshop staff became the key factor in keeping the trams running, but they were unable to prevent breakdowns reaching unacceptable levels. Drivers were instructed to bring trams to a halt using hand brakes only, to reduce the strain on motors. In an attempt to reduce motor wear, bogie car 8 and trailer cars 116-7/21/6/38 were experimentally fitted with air brakes.

In 1917 fuel rationing was introduced forcing the IMB to reduce the number of passenger trains it operated, in order to conserve coal stocks for the ambulance trains. By the end of the year, with most of the stocks depleted, the IMB ceased operating altogether. *Lok* 3 was sent to work on the Trento - Male line in the South Tirol, but it never returned as the province became part of Italy at the end of the war. The Stb's situation was just as serious, for once the supply of spare parts became exhausted, defective cars were withdrawn and serviceable motors and equipment removed to keep others running. Towards the end of the war, with only one motor car in running order, the two remaining steam locomotives were borrowed from the IMB. When the war was over and with the supply of coal increasing, the locomotives were returned to the IMB and the line to Igls reopened.

The first incident to involve a tram at one of the two railway crossings on route 4, occurred on 2 January 1918 when a steam train collided with motor car 5 at the Loretto crossing. Although the car was badly damaged, it was rebuilt after the war. As the subsequent investigation found that the crossing barrier had been inadvertently left open, conductresses were instructed to alight from their trams on arrival at the crossing and check that there were no approaching trains, before giving a lusty blast on their whistle when it was safe for the tram to proceed.

Peace returns

When hostilities ceased on 7 November 1918 the LBIHiT's attention focused on returning its services to their pre-war standards. Route 2 was extended at its northern end to Mühlau and route 4 returned to its southern terminus at Berg Isel. In early 1919, the service frequency on route 3 was improved and trailer operation retained. Safety was not forgotten either. As a result of the accident at Loretto crossing, coloured lights were installed at this and the crossing in Leopoldstrasse; **red** = stop; **green** = go; **white** = overhead power is on.

As the special trackwork into Pradl hospital and at the two railway stations was now redundant, it was lifted and used to double some of the remaining single track sections and replace the last vignoles rails.

Another serious accident occurred on 6 January 1920 involving a fully laden LBIHiT two-car tram, carrying hikers who had transferred from a Stubaitalbahn train. It ran-away while descending the Arlbergbahn viaduct ramp and derailed at speed by the Egger-Lienz-Strasse/Andreas-Hofer-Strasse junction. Trailer 146 careered across the road and crashed into the steps of Hotel Veldidena, sustaining serious damage. One passenger was killed, several seriously injured and car 146 was later rebuilt, but the cause of the accident was never ascertained.

New circular route

One of the busiest periods of the working day was between 15:00 and 18:00 when workers made their way from the city centre to the main station. To bolster the existing tram services the LBIHiT introduced a circular service on 27 June 1923, running as route 0, and operated with two solo 2-axle motor cars. From a starting point at Landesgericht it ran via Anichstrasse, Maria-Theresien-Strasse and Museumstrasse to Süd Tiroler Platz and via Maximilianstrasse back to Landesgericht, but was withdrawn on 15 August after only two months in service. Fluctuations in passenger loadings, however, saw the section from Landesgericht to Brunecker Strasse reinstated as route 5 on several occasions during the next few years.

Having failed with yet another bid to take over the IMB, the LBIHiT was granted a concession to operate a through service of IMB trailers between Berg Isel and Süd Tiroler Platz from 10 July 1924. This was accomplished by uncoupling two of the trailers from the inbound train at Berg Isel and attaching them to a 2-axle LBIHiT motor car. The reformed tramset then followed a circular route via Anichstrasse — Maria-Theresien-Strasse — Museumstrasse — Süd Tiroler Platz — Maximilianstrasse — Andreas-Hofer-Strasse. Back at Berg Isel the procedure was reversed and the trailers coupled to an IMB train for the journey up to Igls. A similar arrangement for through running of trailers from the Stb was not possible because of the limited clearances on the Arlbergbahn viaduct.

The task of clearing snow from the tracks was greatly eased following the purchase of a redundant snowbroom from Wien. Following re-gauging by Simmering Waggonfabrik, it arrived in Innsbruck on 1 November 1925 just in time for the first snows of the winter.

Railcar evaluation on the Stb

The introduction of a competing service by an entrepreneurial bus operator, Leo Bayr, between Innsbruck city centre and Fulpmes via the Brennerstrasse high road, had a serious impact on passenger loadings on the Stubaitalbahn. In a determined effort to prevent further losses, the AGStb requested of the LBIHiT that it provided a special tram service to connect with the Stb trains when they arrived at the Stubaitalbahnhof. When its request was rejected, the Board began an evaluation of alternative methods of extending its service into the city. In 1926 various vehicles were tested, culminating in the purchase of a Perl petrol-driven railcar, similar to the type used by the ÖBB engineering department.

This hybrid vehicle was, in effect, an open-top motor car mounted on flanged-wheels, and was powered by a four-cylinder 14-hp engine. It could carry six passengers plus a driver and had a top speed of 60 km/h — 40 km/h in reverse! A mechanical foot brake operated on the two rear wheels and a hand brake on both front and rear axles. An ingenious hand operated hydraulic jack was built into the chassis to enable it to be lifted and turned at the termini.

Trial running commenced on 27 April 1926 and continued through May and June. It entered revenue earning service on 2 July on a single duty which departed from Maria-Theresien-Strasse at 14:15; the journey to Fulpmes taking just over an hour. But, for reasons believed to be technical in nature, the authorities banned the vehicle from the city's streets only eight weeks later. Seeing this as a possible solution for its spiralling operating costs the car made a series of test runs for the IMB between Berg Isel and Igls, but these were not successful and the option was not pursued. After languishing in the depot for two years, it was dusted off for use as a private-hire vehicle particularly for people wishing to sample the delights of the fresh mountain air. It also saw limited use as transport for the mobility-impaired before being scrapped in 1939.

The appointment of a new director for the AGStb encouraged the Board to take over full responsibility for its railway, and it was soon seeking suitable methods of extending its

The efficiency with which the winters snows were cleared from the tracks was greatly improved following the purchase of this snowbroom from Wien in 1925. Dating from 1906 it was numbered 200 in 1984. *(collection Mackinger)*

The driver sits proudly behind the dash of his Perl petrol-engined railcar as it pauses for the camera at Nockhofweg in 1926. Intended for through running into the city, the vehicle was a dismal failure and spent most of its life in the depot.

(collection Mackinger)

services into the city centre. The Ministry of Trade and Transport proposed a route, running via Leopoldstrasse and Bundesbahnstrasse to the Karwendelbahn platform in Hauptbahnhof, for which it was prepared to pay a proportion of the construction costs. This was acceptable to the Board, but the financial crisis of the early 'thirties prevented its construction.

To cater for the growing number of walkers in the Stubai valley a new halt called Telfeser Wiesen was opened, close to the highest and most scenic part of the line on 27 July 1926. One of the most popular excursions on a summer day was (and still is) to take the tram to Telfeser Wiesen and follow one of the parallel tracks to Telfes (4 km) or Fulpmes (6 km), and catch a tram back to Innsbruck. A siding for goods wagons was installed at the halt for the transfer of produce and agricultural machinery to and from the nearby meadows.

Replacement of the ageing electrical equipment at the Sillwerk power station in 1926 enabled the line voltage to be increased to 3 kV ac, 50 Hz, allowing the trains to run at a slightly faster pace.

Fulpmes station enjoyed a tranquil setting for many years, located as it was on the outskirts of the village. This view looking north towards Telfes, gives a good impression of the type of overhead equipment installed on the Stubaitalbahn during the inter-war period.

(collection Mackinger)

4. Consolidation and the end of steam

The LBIHiT finally took over control of the IMB on 1 January 1927 and soon began planning for the electrification and extension of the line through Igls to the lower station of the *Patscherkofelbahn* (PKB) cable car line; the construction of which was about to begin. But when financial backing could not be obtained the plans were shelved, and the steam locomotives prepared for a further period of service.

Much of the heavy equipment required to construct the PKB was transported up the Igls line using a purpose-built 8-axle trailer, which temporarily incorporated the trucks from goods wagons 203-4. A spur was laid into Westbahnhof goods yard, and a pair of motor cars assigned to shunt the trailer to Berg Isel depot for its onward journey to Igls.

The end of the Igls line?

Improvements made to the Igls line rolling stock were not sufficient to prevent an exodus of passengers to a competing bus service. With dwindling receipts, increasing overheads and worn out track the LBIHiT decided to close the line, and the last passenger trains ran on 1 October 1928. The rolling stock was stored in Berg Isel depot and the track left *in situ* to await a decision on its future.

eastern provinces not changing until June 1935. Apart from limited track alterations, this change had little impact on the tramway as the fleet was double-ended with passenger access from either side.

With an easing of the pressure on the LBIHiT finances, the line to Igls was reopened for passenger services on 15 April 1930. *Lok 2*, fuelled by a cheaper type of coal imported from the Ruhr, had the honour of hauling the first train up the mountainside, and the 30-year old carriages were spruced-up for an occasion many thought would not happen.

Experimentation

As passenger loadings saw significant increases during the summer of 1930, the LBIHiT introduced the following route changes on 1 July:

1B: **Berg Isel** to **Hauptbahnhof** via Maria-Theresien-Strasse, Museumstrasse and Brunecker Strasse.

1H: **Hungerburgbahn** to **Hauptbahnhof** via Ing.-Etzel-Strasse and Brunecker Strasse.

3: Alternate cars extended south from **Wiltener Platz** via Leopoldstrasse to **Berg Isel**.

During the final years of steam operation by the IMB, the canvas screens on the trailer cars were replaced with wooden-framed glazed screens as can be seen in this ca1930 photograph. Lok 2 is about depart Berg Isel with a train for Igls. (W.Kreutz)

On the urban system, route 5 began operating a shuttle service between Landesgericht and Brunecker Strasse via Salurner Strasse and Hbf from 1 May to 8 October 1928 and again from 30 March 1929. A few months later it was extended via Museumstrasse — Maria-Theresien-Strasse — Anichstrasse and Andreas-Hofer-Strasse to Westbahnhof.

At about this time, Austria decided to change the Rule of the Road from left to right, but in two phases; starting with the western provinces. This included Tirol which changed to right-hand rule on 2 April 1930; the

Route 1 was operated in two halves to provide direct links with Hauptbahnhof. In October, when most of the tourists had departed, routes 1 and 3 reverted to their winter schedules and the short workings were withdrawn. These same changes were reinstated in 1931 and again with the advent of the Second World War.

In May 1932, bogie car 4 was fitted with new controllers and 4 x 36.8-kW motors to evaluate its potential for operation on route 4. During testing it was determined that the journey between Wiltener Platz and Hall could be reduced by 6 minutes with the car hauling

Route 3 was diverted through the Triumphpforte to a terminus at Wiltener Platz in 1923 and a decade later, cars 44 and 45 glide their way through ankle-deep snow in Leopoldstrasse. At that time, a single track under the archway was used by cars in both directions. (W.Kreutz)

Apart from the track, very little has changed in this part of Rennweg since motor car 41 was photographed in the early 1920s. Although route 2 closed in 1926 the track remained in use by cars on route 4 until 1939. (W.Kreutz)

Route 5 was introduced to cover the busiest section of withdrawn route 0, between Museumstrasse and Landesgericht via Salurner Strasse in 1924 and was extended to Westbahnhof in 1929. Car 38 is waiting to cross the junction at Triumphpforte, 24-07-26. (W.Kreutz)

To cope with increased summer passenger loadings on route 1 the route was divided into two in 1930 and operated with extra cars. Route 1B ran between Berg Isel and Hauptbahnhof and 1H between the latter and Hungerburgbahn. A two-car set on a 1H duty turns from Salurner Strasse into Südtiroler Platz during that first summer. (W.Kreutz)

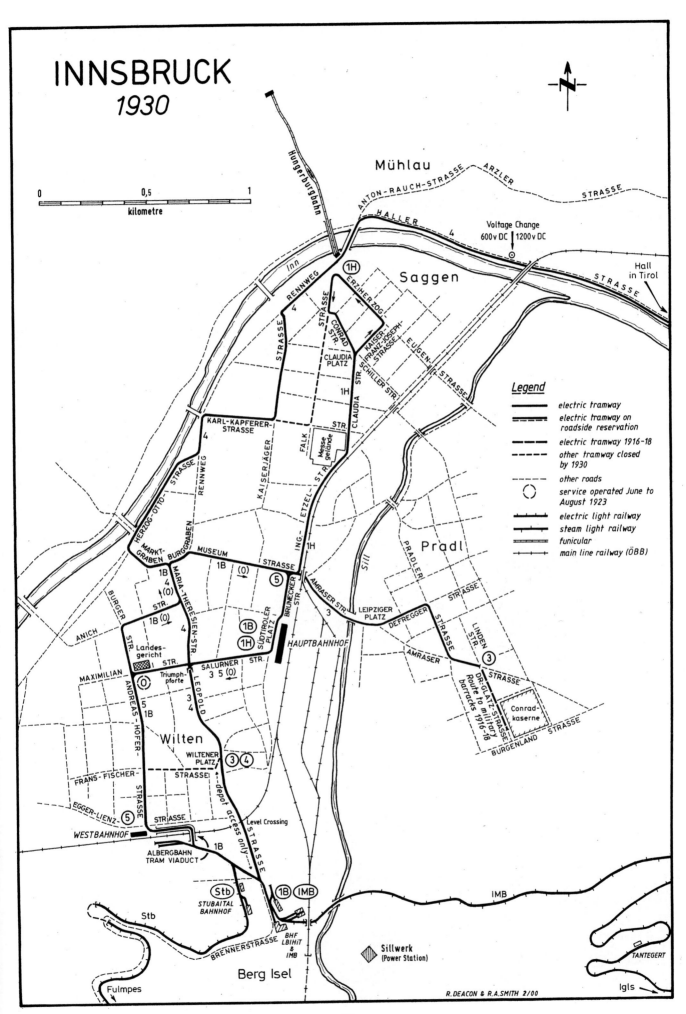

INNSBRUCK
1930

Mühlau

Saggen

Pradl

Wilten

Berg Isel

Legend

electric tramway

electric tramway on roadside reservation

electric tramway 1916-18

other tramway closed by 1930

other roads

service operated June to August 1923

electric light railway

steam light railway

funicular

main line railway (ÖBB)

Voltage Change 600 v DC | 1200 v DC

Hall in Tirol

Hungerburgbahn

ANTON-RAUCH-STRASSE

ARZLER STRASSE

HALLER STRASSE

Inn

RENNWEG

STRASSE

ERZHERZOG- STRASSE

CONRAD STR.

CLAUDIA PLATZ

KAISER- FRANZ-JOSEPH- STRASSE

SCHILLER STR.

EUGEN- STRASSE

CLAUDIA STR.

KARL-KAPFERER- STRASSE

KAISERJÄGER STR.

FALK STR.

Messe gelände

HERZOG-OTTO- STRASSE

RENNWEG

BURGGRABEN

MARKT- GRABEN

MUSEUM STRASSE

BURGER STR.

ANICH STR.

MARIA-THERESIEN-STR.

MAXIMILIAN STR.

ANDREAS-HOFER- STRASSE

Landes- gericht

STR.

Triumph- pforte

SÜDTIROLER PLATZ

BRUNECKER STR.

ING.-ETZEL- STR.

Sill

AMRASER STR.

LEIPZIGER PLATZ

DEFREGGER STR.

PRADLER STRASSE

AMRASER STRASSE

LINDEN STR.

DR.GLATZ-STRASSE

BURGENLAND STRASSE

Conrad- kaserne

Route to military barracks 1916-18

HAUPTBAHNHOF

SALURNER STR.

LEOPOLD STRASSE

WILTENER PLATZ

FRANS-FISCHER- STRASSE

EGGER-LIENZ- STRASSE

STRASSE

WESTBAHNHOF

ALBERGBAHN TRAM VIADUCT

depot access only

Level Crossing

STRASSE

BRENNERSTRASSE

Stb

STUBAITAL BAHNHOF

Fulmpes

BHF LBIHIT & IMB

IMB

Sillwerk (Power Station)

IMB

TANTEGERT

Igls

R.DEACON & R.A.SMITH 2/00

0   0,5   1
kilometre

1H

1H

1B

(O)

5

1B

4

(O)

1B (O)

4

1B

(O)

1B

1H

3 5 (O)

3

4

5

1B

3

3 4

5

1B

Stb

1B

IMB

4

four trailers, and by 10 minutes when running solo; an improvement deemed sufficient to warrant similar modifications to sister cars 2-3/7-8 during their next overhauls. Cars 1/5-6 received new electrical equipment in 1941 but retained their two-motor configurations.

The end of steam operation

To assess the viability of using the bogie cars on the Igls line, re-motored Hall car 4 and four ballasted trailers undertook a series of tests on the Stubaitalbahn in 1933 using a temporary 1200 volts dc supply. The set covered the 6 kilometres to Mutters in 13 minutes, 7 minutes quicker than the ac cars. Suitably impressed, the LBIHiT applied to the transport ministry for financial assistance towards the cost of converting the line for electric traction.

Two years later, on 30 October 1935, the government authorised credits of ÖS 200 000 to enable the work to commence (the *Österreichische Schilling* had replaced the Krone in 1925). As luck would have it, AEG was in urgent need of work and offered to manage the project at no cost on condition that all contracts were

placed with the company. The widening of the Ambras tunnel to accommodate the Hall bogie cars was put in hand, and in order to keep costs to a minimum the overhead equipment was erected on wooden masts cut from the local forests. Four, more powerful, 52.5-kW motors were fitted to bogie car 3, and the ex-IMB trailer cars 101-6 were modified to work with electric traction.

The electrification proceeded at a fast pace allowing test running to start on 12 June 1936, and crew training to be completed in record time. On 28 June, electric trams replaced the steam locomotives when car 3, liberally decorated with flowers and bunting, departed from Berg Isel to the echoes of a brass band. From the same date, the line was incorporated in the urban tramway timetable as route 6. *Lok 1* was sold to the light railway at Sylt in Germany, but there is no record of what became of *Lok 2*.

Inevitably there were problems, the most serious of these being the difficulty encountered by drivers when applying three different types of braking system; air, solenoid and hand, on the downhill section. Conductors

(above) With the overhead masts and equipment in place, IMB Lok 2 has only a few more weeks to haul its heavy loads through the Patschberg forest to Igls, and judging by the precariously placed pushchairs on the water tank, the train must have been full. (J.O. Slezak) On 28 June, 1936, electric power replaced steam and decorated Hall car 3 crosses the river Sill (left) during its inaugural run to Igls as new route 6. Some rush-hour services were subsequently extended to Maria-Theresien-Strasse.   (W.Kreutz)

risked life and limb jumping between the bucking trailers to adjust the handbrakes on each car. Maximum speeds on the steepest section of the line were set at 30 km/h when running uphill, and 25 km/h for the downward run. The journey time to Igls was scheduled for 21 minutes with 23 minutes allowed for the return trip. Motor cars 3 and 4, modified trailer cars 101-6 and works cars 201-4/52/62-3 were the only vehicles permitted on the line.

During 1937, trailer cars 102/6/18/21/3/41 were extensively rebuilt and their braking systems modified as they passed through overhaul. A redesigned saloon incorporating two large arch-shaped windows distinguished them from the rest of the fleet, several more of which were subsequently rebuilt to the same specification.

Apart from the open summer cars, the 2-axle trailer cars delivered by Graz between 1891 and 1900 were fitted with four-window saloons and clerestory roofs. During 1937/8, several were rebuilt with twin arched-shaped windows as depicted in this picture of car 119. (A. Luft)

Dual-voltage supply

Routes 4 and 6 at Innsbruck were dual-voltage with a rather crude semi-automatic changeover system. Route 4 had a 600-volt dc supply as far as Mühlau, and a 1200-volt supply between Mühlau and Solbad Hall. The section between Mühlau and Hall had a level crossing with the mainline railway, and when this was electrified (at 15 kV) the section of overhead at the crossing, normally "dead ", could be switched to railway or tramway voltage as appropriate; however, this was done with suitable safety precautions only when a train or tram was stuck on the "dead" section. Route 6 to Igls was steeply graded, so the greater part of the route was fed at 1200 volts after electrification in 1936, with a comparatively short section at Berg Isel at the urban supply of 600 volts.

In effect, each of the motor cars 1-8 had two alternative circuits, one for each voltage. For two-motor cars, the motors were normally (1200 V) connected in series, while four-motor cars were normally connected in series-pairs. On the 600-volt sections, the motors or motor-pairs would be connected in pairs-parallel. The voltage changeover switch would also select the connection of the individual lamps and heaters to match the available supply. The switchgear on these trams was so arranged that, on safety grounds, when the overhead supply was interrupted, the changeover contactor would normally drop into the 1200 volts position. Thus, on route, the railway crossings would never require any action by the driver or conductor beyond vigorous coasting across the "dead" sections. Action was needed only at the voltage step-down points when running into the city. It is unclear whether the voltage switch would have to be operated at supply breaks in the urban area, or whether it

Hall bogie car 3 was to spend 35 years of its operating life on route 6. Here it climbs passed Schloss Ambras and Tummelplatz en-route for Igls in 1936. (collection Mackinger)

would be left in the 600-volt position. The location of the voltage changeover point on route 4 was at Mühlau and by the Sill Brücke on route 6.

Whereas cars 1-8 were all dual-voltage, it is unclear whether only four-motor cars could have worked on route 6. Equally obscure is whether cars 61 and 62 (purchased after World War II) were also re-wired as dual-voltage cars; there are statements that this was the intention, but the confusion arises from a statement that Siemens modified the cars for 800 volts, which does not make sense, either for running on 600 or 1200 volts.

Typical scenes on the Stubaitalbahn are captured in these views of a Fulpmes-bound train on the steady climb south of Gärberbach (above), and the Stb station and depot buildings at Berg Isel (below). The little-used track connecting with the urban system is just visible by the embankment on the left. *(collection Mackinger)*

5. Invasion, World War 2 and Integration

Annexation

As the clouds of war hung menacingly across the continent of Europe, Mussolini passed through the Brenner Pass and Innsbruck on his way to meet Hitler to put the final touches to their master plan. On 13 March 1938, German troops marched into Austria and annexed the country. On 5 April, Hitler visited Innsbruck to make a speech, for which the central area of the city was completely sealed off. Four days later, he announced that Austria was part of the Third Reich. Travel restrictions were introduced which barred people from using public transport without valid identification papers, currency restrictions were imposed and the *Österreichische Schilling* was replaced by the *German ReichMark* (RM).

Military uniforms are much in evidence on motor car 54 as it hauls trailer 144 through the streets in Saggen on a route 1 service to Berg Isel. *(W.Kreutz)*

Trolleybus proposal

The first real threat to abandon the trams occurred during 1938 when an anti-tram lobby in the Council proposed that trolleybuses should replace the trams on route 3. Increasing passenger loadings from the expanding military establishments and the inability of the trams to cope, together with the cost and upheaval of doubling the remaining single track sections in Pradl, were cited as valid reasons. Trolleybuses, it was maintained, would provide a cheaper and more efficient service, but a sceptical LBIHiT ordered a review of its Pradl services. It reported that doubling of the single track sections would cost half that needed to convert the route to trolleybus operation, and so the proposal was rejected.

Unperturbed, the anti-tram faction suggested that trolleybuses should be used to replace the trams on route 4 to Hall, but the Council was not convinced and the proposal was once again rejected. Four years later, however, trolleybuses did find favour in Innsbruck, but as an addition to and not as a replacement for the trams.

As construction of a new road bridge at Mühlau (a replacement for the Kettenbrücke) progressed, alterations to the routing of traffic through the northeast suburbs were put into force, with Rennweg becoming a major access route for motor vehicles. In July 1939, tram route 4 was diverted over the tracks of route 1 at the Hungerburgbahn to run via Museumstrasse, Maria-Theresien-Strasse and Leopoldstrasse to Wiltener Platz. The tracks in Rennweg were lifted and used to double some of the single track sections on route 3.

World War 2

The strict financial controls imposed by the German government prevented the purchase of new rolling stock, but permission to acquire three, veteran, 2-axle motor cars from Remscheid was forthcoming. The policy of buying second-hand tramcars was thus begun and has, with a few exceptions, been adhered to ever since. Built in 1903 by Falkenried, and mounted on two single-axle radial trucks, they were fitted with similar AEG electrical equipment to the Innsbruck cars, but their couplers were incompatible with the rest of the fleet. Larger than the Innsbruck standard car type (nos. 32-54), they had a capacity for 22 seated and 25 standing passengers. Following repainting, they received fleet numbers 13-15 and were put into service on route 3 during the early months of 1940. For most of their active lives, they were utilised on this route and as peak-hour extras.

Radial-truck car 13 was acquired from Remscheid in 1939 and put to work on route 3 to Pradl, where this photograph was taken in September 1940. *(W.Kreutz)*

The first serious tramway accident for many years occurred during a blizzard on 22 December 1940 on the Igls line. Winding its way up through the woods towards Tantegert, car 7, with four fully-laden trailers, collided head-on with a five-car set headed by car 2 returning to the city. Several passengers and both drivers were seriously injured. The motor cars had recently been overhauled and re-equipped with four motors and were badly damaged, and three trailers on the down-tramset sustained minor damage when they derailed. Blame for the accident was apportioned to the controller who gave permission for the down-tram to leave Tantegert. Three weeks later, Hall bogie car 6 ploughed into the side of a coal train in thick fog at the Loretto railway crossing; the

On 22 December, 1940, a collision occurred between two trains in woods to the north of Tantegert station causing serious damage to both bogie cars, numbers 2 and 7, and derailment of three trailers on the inbound train. Both cars were repaired by prisoners of war and returned to service. (G. Mayr)

The final year of operations by the LBIHiT is depicted in these two photographs.
(left) Motor car 46 and trailer 132 were caught during a layover in Berg Isel depot while operating on route 1. Four years later, the motor car was badly damaged in an air raid and after many years in store, was rebuilt as trailer car 145. (below) Motor car 41 runs round trailer 127 at the Wiltener Platz terminus of route 3. The trailer was one of four open summer cars that received fully enclosed saloons during the war.
(W.Kreutz)

force of the impact derailing a coal wagon and causing serious damage to the tram. The subsequent investigation found that the crossing barrier had been inadvertently left up following a nearby road accident.

Cars 1 and 5 were fitted with two 61.5-kW Siemens motors in order to provide cover on the Igls route during the absence of the damaged cars which were repaired by prisoners-of-war.

In 1941, as the supply of petrol became constrained, fuel rationing was imposed on motorists, and by the end of the year the same restrictions were extended to public transport. Several bus routes were suspended, mostly those running close to the tram routes, and the seasonal tram route 1H was reintroduced as route E to provide relief on route 1. As passenger loadings on the trams rose by 50%, extra capacity was provided by rebuilding the open trailer cars with fully enclosed saloons.

Severe restrictions were also imposed on the Stubaitalbahn, at the outbreak of the Second World War, causing a rapid deterioration in both track and rolling stock. Minor derailments became commonplace, although damage to both vehicles and passengers was seldom serious. Nevertheless, the situation was bad enough for the Council to provide finance for the overhaul of the motor cars and the purchase of second-hand trackwork and equipment; much of which came from railways which had been forced to close.

Innsbrucker Verkehrsbetriebe AG (IVB)

27 October 1941 was an historic day for public transport in Innsbruck, when the bus and tram services operated by the LBIHiT and AGStb were amalgamated to form a new LBIHiT board members. Called the Innsbrucker

In the same raid, motor car 54 and trailer 145 were both destroyed under the rubble of a collapsing building by the Burggraben/Museumstrasse junction. Serviceable equipment was recovered, and parts from 54 were used to rebuild damaged sister car 40 which was renumbered 54. It too survived the ravages of time to become an exhibit in the Zeughaus Museum in the city. Berg Isel depot suffered direct hits on the controller's office, crew rooms and passenger waiting rooms, and damage to tracks and overhead around other parts of the city caused major disruption to services. Fortunately, the trams escaped serious damage.

The story of how the IVB came to acquire bogie car 60 and the dates on which specific events occurred are unclear. The most plausible version is that in 1942 Italian manufacturing company Breda, based in Milano,

A third air raid on 13 June, 1944, caused extensive damage to Berg Isel depot and several tramcars. Visible among the debris are motor car 36 and trailer 109. (W.Kreutz)

Verkehrsbetriebe AG (Innsbruck Transport Service), it is still the responsible body for running public transport in the city.

Maintaining the trams in a serviceable condition was the immediate priority of the IVB. To provide a source of spare parts, two redundant 2-axle motor cars – numbers 2 and 4 – were obtained from Pirmasens in Germany in July 1943, the electrical equipment removed and the bodies scrapped

Allied bombing

The comparative tranquillity, which for so long had enshrined Innsbruck, was shattered on 15 December 1943 when the first of a score of allied bombing raids shook the city. On the corner formed by Andreas-Hofer-Strasse and Egger-Lienz-Strasse, the blast from a bomb lifted motor car 39 and trailer 142 clear of the tracks and sucked them under the masonry from a collapsing building. The motor car was badly damaged and scrapped, but the trailer was rebuilt and later preserved.

had completed an order for a batch of six double-ended bogie motor cars for Beograd but delivery was blocked by the German administrator in Yugoslavia. Five of the cars were modified for use on the Genova system in 1943, and the sixth sold to the IVB a year later where it entered service in an attractive two-tone green livery as car 60 on 2 July 1944.

The vehicle was built to the latest Italian streamline styling, with double-folding, power-operated doors at each end. There were 26 reversible seats for passengers plus a seat at each end for the driver. It was originally equipped with trolleypoles, but these were replaced by a pantograph before the car entered service. At the time it was the most advanced car in Austria and included automatic acceleration with 2 x 165 steps in its switchgear. The driver had a simple controller with seven notches; electric brake, off, slow speed (for shunting), plus one series and three parallel notches. Normal braking was a combination of light rheostatic and air while electro-magnetic brakes would be used in an emergency.

Two more air raid casualties stand forlornly in the centre of Maria-Theresien-Strasse while piles of rubble lie all around. Every window in motor car 45 and the trailer have be blown out by the blast.
(W.Kreutz)

The appearance of a brand new, ultra-modern tram in sparkling green and white livery, has grabbed the attention of passengers on the back of route 4 trailer car 116, on the occasion of the car's first test run in 1944. Fitted with automatic acceleration control equipment and no less than five braking system, bogie car 60 was the pride of the fleet for many years.
(G. Mayr)

During the night of 20 October 1944 the city suffered another air raid, an experience that would increase in intensity over the next six months. On this occasion the track and overhead were damaged in Andreas-Hofer-Strasse, Berg Isel depot was hit again, with damage to buildings and two motor cars, and a conductress was seriously injured. Tram routes 1 and 3 were suspended and shuttle services operated on the outer sections of routes 4 and 6, until repairs allowed the gradual resumption of normal services. To minimise the effects of the bombing, all four Stb motor cars and three passenger trailers were sheltered in the tunnel under the Brennerstrasse overnight. Minor damage was, however, sustained by trailers 11/5-6 and goods wagons 21/5-7/34-6, and over 500 metres of track was completely destroyed by stray bombs in the Kreith area.

When American forces entered Innsbruck on 5 May 1945, 2.3 km of the urban system's track and 5.6 km of overhead was out of use, as was the Loretto railway crossing, the Arlbergbahn tram viaduct, the bridge over the Sillkanal and some facilities at Berg Isel depot. Several trams were badly damaged and three motor cars (39/45/54) and six passenger trailers (101/7/27/32/4/45) had been destroyed.

6. Peace and Independence

The aftermath

The return to peace allowed the wartime restrictions to be gradually eased, and a 48-hour week and the *Österreichische Schilling* reinstated. The French were given responsibility of occupying the Tirol as the countries of Europe tried once again to settle their differences over the negotiating table.

Of more immediate concern to the IVB was the availability of sufficient rolling stock with which to restart its services. As the Hall bogie cars had escaped damage, routes 4 and 6 were able to resume normal service quite quickly, but with shortages of vital materials and equipment it was left to the ingenuity of the Berg Isel staff, using parts removed from bomb damaged cars, to carry out repairs. Several 2-axle trailers received major rebuilds during the process, sometimes taking the fleet numbers from the donor vehicles, and a few motor cars were also renumbered following a reshuffle of bodies, trucks and electrical equipment.

Although the Stb motor cars escaped the bombing unscathed they were often out of service through lack of spare parts, and two were temporary withdrawn to provide a source of spares. When one of these was returned to service at the end of 1947, the pre-war timetable was reinstated.

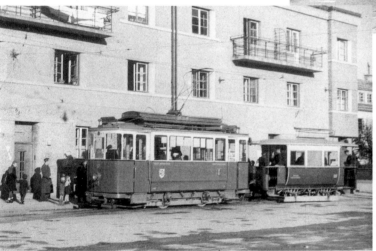

Former Winterthur motor car 17 and trailer 133 are seen here on route 3 at Dr.-Glatz-Strasse in October 1947. Note that the trailer has been fitted with a temporary wooden panel in the centre window. (W.Kreutz)

During the same year, the town of Hall was presented with a 2-axle motor car as a gesture of good will by its Swiss partner town Winterthur. Built by SLM in Winterthur in 1915 its 600 volt dc electrical system prevented it being used on the eastern section of the Hall line, so it was passed on to a grateful IVB which put it to work on route 3, still bearing its original fleet number, 17.

Considering that the Stubaitalbahn comprised single track with numerous curves and no signals there were remarkably few incidents until that is, on 18 September 1948 when an extraordinary accident occurred. A Fulpmes bound train suffered a motor failure shortly after leaving Gärberbach, and the crew decided to coast slowly back to Innsbruck without informing the controller who had, in the meantime, authorised the departure of a motor car on a test run to Mutters. A collision occurred in which trailers 11-12 and a goods wagon were derailed and the braking system on the test car sustained a leak. Gathering speed

it ran back down the line and through the Stubaitalbahnhof before crashing through the buffers and into Pastorstrasse. Amazingly, there were few injuries and only minor damage was caused to the motor car. The plush second-class seating and panoramic windows on stored car 4 were replaced with standard fittings and the car prepared for service.

Replacement cars

The rolling stock shortage continued to intensify as the ageing fleet became less reliable. Cars 42 and 50 were scrapped in 1949/50 and serviceable equipment used to refurbish 43 which was renumbered 50, but as there was not enough spare equipment to repair sister car 46, it was

(above) One of the Berg Isel depot staff winds-on the handbrake of trailer 145 during a fly-shunting manoeuvre with motor car 21. The trailer was built from the remnants of motor car 46 in 1952 because of a lack of spare electrical equipment.

(collection Mackinger)

rebuilt as a trailer and renumbered 145 to replace that lost in the war. New 39.75-kW Elin motors were fitted to cars 47-51 as they passed through overhaul, however.

During this period, some of the tramways in Switzerland had begun to dispose of their older vehicles and replace them with the new "Swiss Standard" tram. As the IVB could not afford to buy new trams it purchased eight 1898-built 2-axle motor cars and seven 1908-built 2-axle trailers from Basel in 1950. These were in excellent condition and the only modifications carried out in Berg Isel comprised removal of the clerestory roofs and full partitioning of the platforms on the motor cars. Originally numbered 24/26/27/32/29 /34/31/37 in Basel, the motor cars were renumbered 25-31 respectively and car 37 became a source of spare parts. The centre-entrance trailer cars, ex-Basel 282/4/6-9/93, were renumbered 151-7 respectively. Seven tram-sets were formed and they entered service, still in their green Basel livery, on the Pradl route allowing ex-Remscheid cars 13-15 to be scrapped.

Another motor car (41) and three more trailer cars (290-2) were purchased from Basel in 1952, and these were renumbered 32 and 158-160 respectively. The original IVB motor car 32 had been scrapped by this time, and the body from sister car 37 transferred to car 48 to produce a new car 48. Parts from scrapped cars were also used to build a *new* 2-axle trailer to the same design as the 1906 batch (142-4), and this was numbered 148. This was very much a period of make-do-and-mend.

During the early fifties, a large number of second-hand cars were obtained from different systems. From Basel came nine motor cars and ten centre entrance trailers and these entered service in the green Basel livery between 1950 and 1958. Seen here (above, left and right) are motor car 31 at Berg Isel and trailer 155 at Wiltener Platz operating on route 3. (collection Mackinger/H. Potschener). While these were a considerable success, the opposite was true for the twelve cars obtained from Thun, two photographs of which are shown below. (left) STJ motor car 3 standing in the open at Berg Isel depot, never entered service in Innsbruck (ETB), while motor car 61 seen heading a three car set (right) comprising trailers 161 and 162 lasted just four days. It is seen on a test run on route 4 near Hungerburgbahn in 1953. (W.Kreutz)

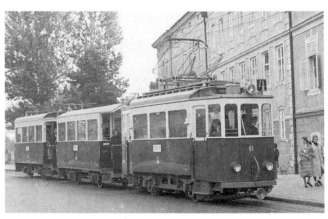

The four cars donated by the city of Zürich to the Innsbruck in 1954 were an unqualified success and were a regular sight on route 1 until the late seventies. Here, motor car 20 and Basel trailer 152 have just arrived at the Hungerburgbahn terminus of route 1. (J.O. Slezak)

To enable the construction of Konzert Brücke, the Arlberg tram viaduct was closed on 25 January 1956. A makeshift terminus was installed in Egger-Lienz-Strasse while temporary tracks were laid across a piece of open land known as Schrebergarten to complete the route 1 link with Berg Isel. (left) Motor car 48 and matching trailer run over the viaduct (G. Mayr), while (below, left) motor car 21 shunts around trailer 152 at the makeshift terminus and (below, right), motor car 50 and trailer 148 cross on the passing loop installed in Schrebergarten (W.Kreutz). On 15 August, the Schrebergarten trackwork was lifted and trams diverted to run over the new bridge.

The increasing number of passengers now using route 4 inspired a further visit to Switzerland in the spring of 1953; this time to inspect withdrawn rolling stock on the Rechtsüfrige Thunerseebahn (STJ) at the lakeside resort of Thun. Built by Credé of Kassel in 1913, with electrical equipment supplied by Siemens, motor cars 3-4/6/10/2/4 and passenger trailers 31-2/4/52-4 were purchased and transported to Innsbruck; the intention being to use them as two or three car sets on the Hall line. Two motor cars, numbers 4 and 6, were prepared for service and renumbered 62 and 61 respectively, followed by trailer cars 32 and 52 which became 162 and 161.

They were introduced on rush-hour services on route 4, but withdrawn after only four days as they could not keep to the required service speed. An embarrassing *faux-pas* was now realised in that the cars were built for operation using the uncommon voltage of 1100 volts and not the 600 and 1200 volts supplied to the Hall line. The two motor cars were adapted for use as works cars on the Hall and Igls lines where they survived until scrapping in the early 1960s, along with the unused STJ cars. Trailer cars 161-2 were, however, transferred to the Stb where they were used to boost that line's capacity during the increasingly popular skiing seasons

Fifty years young!

On 1 August 1954 the Stubaitalbahn celebrated its fiftieth anniversary, and to mark the occasion festivities were held in the villages served by the line. The character of the railway had hardly changed over the years, the original rolling stock was still giving sterling service and the infrastructure remained very much as built.

To help overcome the setback experienced with the STJ cars, the Verkehrsbetriebe Zürich (VBZ) donated four, fully enclosed, Schlieren-built 2-axle motor cars,

dating from 1907/9, to the IVB. Fitted with Oerlikon electrical equipment they were numbered 144/5/1146/147 in the VBZ fleet and, unlike the STJ cars, performance was not a problem as these were equipped with two 54-kW motors. Before entering service in Innsbruck they were repainted red and white and renumbered 18-21 and were usually coupled with trailer cars 146-7/152-3. Winterthur car 17, however, was scrapped and replaced by Basel motor car 37; the car originally purchased as a source of spares. It received the fleet number 24 and entered service in October 1958.

To provide better connection between Egger-Lienz-Strasse and Pastorstrasse, construction of a new road bridge was begun alongside the Arlbergbahn tram-viaduct, which was closed on 25 January 1956. To enable route 1 cars to continue working through to Berg Isel, a length of sleepered track, complete with passing loop and tram stop, was installed on an open piece of land known as Schrebergarten. When the Konzert Brücke opened on 15 August 1956 the trams were diverted to run over it and the Schrebergarten link removed.

During a violent storm, Hall motor car 5 was blown on its side and seriously damaged. It was taken to the Berg Isel workshops where it was rebuilt as a prototype for the refurbishment of the complete batch. Its matchwood-style body fittings were replaced with flush-fitting sheet-steel panels, and route number boxes — similar to those on the Basel cars — were mounted on the roof ends. Cars 1-4/6-7 were similarly rebuilt during the late 'fifties, but car 8 retained its original form.

New trams at last

The erosion of the motor car fleet continued with the withdrawal of car 36 in 1959, and the poor condition of the remaining cars of this type was causing serious

During the period that route 1 terminated in Egger-Lienz-Strasse, routes 3 and 6 were extended to run between Wiltener Platz and Berg Isel. In this view, Hall car 3 is heading south along Leopoldstrasse with a route 3 car behind.

(W.Kreutz)

panels, white window surrounds with a pronounced "V" on the front dash, a light-grey roof and an abundance of chrome trim. Passengers boarded via a double-door entrance at the rear, purchasing a ticket from a seated conductor as they entered, and alighted from a central pair of doors or a single door by the driver.

Route 1, on which they were destined to operate, already possessed a turning loop at Hungerburgbahn, but this was not the case at Berg Isel where the 2-axle motor cars reversed by shunting round their trailers. A reversing-triangle was installed on the east side of Klostergasse in June 1960 but it saw little use, as a section of single track was laid in Klostergasse to form a loop. The single track link between Berg Isel depot and Wiltener Platz was lifted during 1962, because of its poor condition.

A new rush-hour service was introduced on 1 January 1961 running between Berg Isel and Pradl and, as it traversed sections of both routes 1 and 3, it was given the route number 1/3.

With the arrival of the bogie cars, the last few veteran 2-axle motor cars were withdrawn from regular service in June 1960, but they remained available for rush-hour duties until 22 June 1961 when cars 44/7/9/51/61 and trailer 153 were scrapped. Trailer cars 142-5/151/4-160, on the other hand, were fitted with rail-brakes and compact-couplers to enable them to work with any of the remaining 2-axle motor cars. The withdrawal of obsolete stock continued through 1963 with the disposal for scrap of motor cars 38/48/52/62, leaving just two of the original 2-axle motor cars — car 53 for use as a railgrinder and car 54 for general duties.

Traffic congestion

To resolve growing traffic congestion in the central area, a one-way system was introduced for motor vehicles using Burggraben, Marktgraben and Museumstrasse in May 1963, but this had little impact on the trams which continued to run in both directions. However, the lack of passengers using route 3 between Triumphpforte and the narrow traffic-light controlled

concern. As the IVB's finances were now in a healthier state, an order was placed with the Lohner company of Wien for six single-ended bogie cars *(Grossraumwagen)* to be built under licence from Düwag. The first car, number 61, arrived on 14 June 1960, and after presentation to the press it was put to work on crew training. It entered revenue service on route 1 on 22 July and was joined by cars 62-6 during the following months. These new cars were 13.4 metres long, had seating for 25 passengers with room for 51 standing, and were fitted with Austrian electrical equipment supplied by Elin. The livery comprised bright red waist

The arrival of six new bogie cars in 1960 began the transformation of the IVB system. Car 65 was a year old when photographed turning from Egger-Lienz-Strasse into Fritz-Konzert-Strasse on a route 1 service in September 1961.
(author)

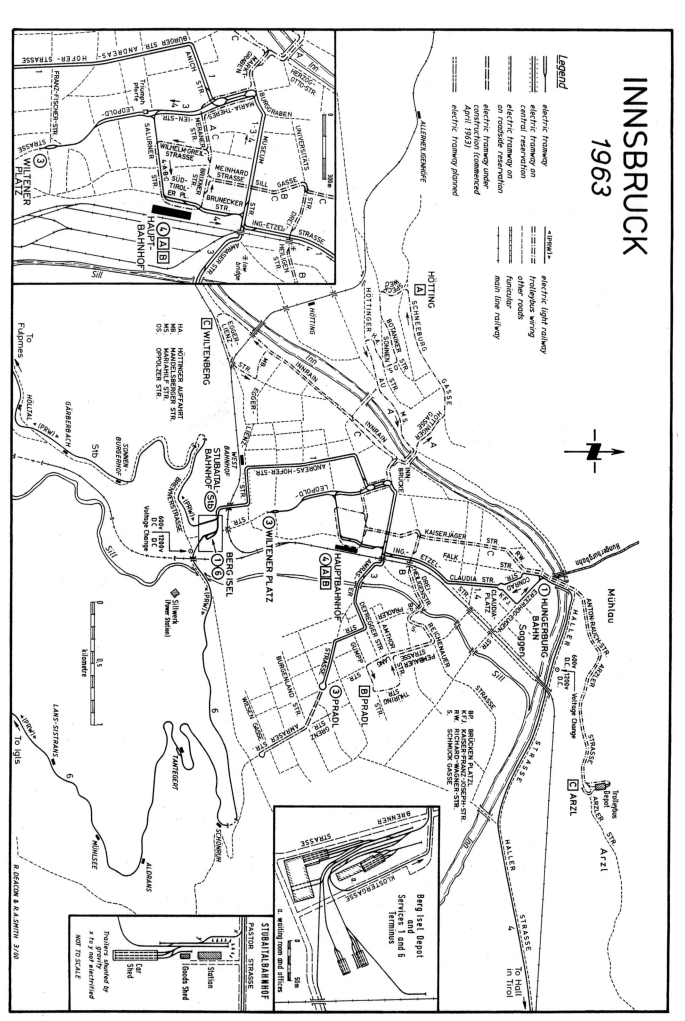

INNSBRUCK 1963

Legend

electric tramway
electric tramway on central reservation
electric tramway on roadside reservation
electric tramway under construction (commenced April 1963)
electric tramway planned

◄(PRW)▶ electric light railway
trolleybus wiring
other roads
funicular
main line railway

R.DEACON & R.A.SMITH 3/00

Stubaitalbahnhof
NOT TO SCALE
Trailers shunted by gravity
x to y not electrified
PASTOR STRASSE
Car Shed
Station
Goods Shed
Waiting room and offices

Berg Isel Depot and Services 1 and 6 terminus
BRENNER STRASSE
KLOSTERGASSE
0   50m

1960 saw the withdrawal of the remaining 2-axle motor cars from the series 32-54. (left) Looking very smart following overhaul, car 51 leads grubby sister cars 50 and 53 away from Maria-Theresien-Strasse on a special service to Amras Friedhof on Allerheiligen day, 01-11-56.   (W.Kreutz)

In this early 'fifties view, motor car 53 is still equipped with a bow collector as it operates a route 1 service in Pastorstrasse with a Merano trailer in tow.   (collection Mackinger)

thoroughfare to Wiltener Platz led to the decision to close this branch, and this occurred on 31 December 1964. On the next day, route 3 was diverted at Triumphpforte to run via the loop formed by Salurner Strasse, Maria-Theresien-Strasse and Museumstrasse. At its other end, a double-track extension was opened from Pradl to Amras on 8 September 1965. In the same year, the name Berg Isel was combined to form a single word, Bergisel.

With 67 years of passenger service behind them, the exiles from Basel were now reaching the end of their working lives, and to replace them, seven 6-axle single-ended articulated cars were ordered from Lohner under licence from Düwag. Numbered 71-77 these cars were 19.4 metres long, with a capacity for 40 seated and 72 standing passengers, and the first car arrived on 29 July 1966. The Basel cars were withdrawn from passenger

service on 8 November and several escaped the scrapman's torch. Motor car 30 and trailer cars 158-160 were sold to a local camp site, and four years later car 30 was sold on to a cafe in Lustenau for use as a bar. Trailer 160 was transferred to the fledgling Eurotram museum group in Klagenfurt in 1977, car 28 became a mobile rest room for track maintenance crews and car 31 was assigned to general duties.

New bodies for old

Using money from a provincial grant, new bodies were built on the trucks of Stb trailer cars 11-16 in the IVB workshops, commencing with car 16 in March 1963. It received a fully-enclosed saloon with five half-drop aluminium-framed windows on either side and 38 varnished pine seats, access from the open balconies

The introduction of the Lohner 6-axle cars brought a much needed improvement to the quality of service offered by the IVB. Here, car 74 has just arrived at Berg Isel with passengers wishing to transfer to a train on route 6 headed by motor car 2 in 1967.
(collection Mackinger)

The Basel cars had operated services on route 3 for 16 years but were now life-expired and withdrawn. (left) Motor car 26 hauls a 150-series trailer passed the Annasäule memorial on a route 3 duty in 1954, while motor car 27 and trailer 153 await their next departure from Dr.-Glatz-Strasse a decade later.
(W.Kreutz)

being gained via sliding doors at each end. The remaining cars passed through the workshops until the last, car 15, was completed in September 1966. The finished vehicle bore a marked resemblance to the 2-axle carriages then running on the Austrian state railways.

To protect trains on the more steeply graded sections of the Stb, more stringent safety regulations were introduced in November 1963. The conductor assigned to the last trailer was given the responsibility for applying the brakes, and a second conductor rode alongside the driver to provide assistance in the event of an emergency. As the bodywork on the ex-STJ trailer cars

161-2 had badly deteriorated the Board decided to scrap them, and construct one new trailer using money left over from the provincial grant. Numbered 17 it was built in the IVB workshops to the same specification as rebodied cars 11-16, and it entered service in April 1967.

Withdrawn in 1971 IVB motor car 54 became an exhibit in the Innsbruck Zeughaus a year later where it was joined by the unnumbered snowbroom and trailer 124. During the year, Zürich motor car 21 was converted into a railgrinder and painted in a distinctive yellow livery as a replacement for railgrinder 53 which, together with trailer 143 and goods wagons 253/63, was obtained by the Tramway Museum group in Graz.

Autobahn threatens the tramway

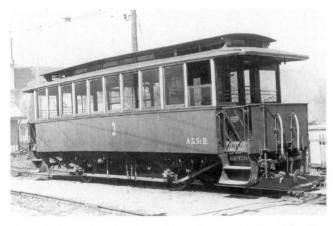

Two photographs showing old and new on the Stb. The American-style body on trailer car 12 (above) was built in 1904 and replaced with a new body to the same design as all-new car 17. (ETB) (below) Construction of new bodies was undertaken in the IVB's own workshops between 1963 and 1967. (collection Mackinger)

Motor car 3 threads its way on new alignment through the autobahn construction works with a train bound for Berg Isel.
(F. Fritz)

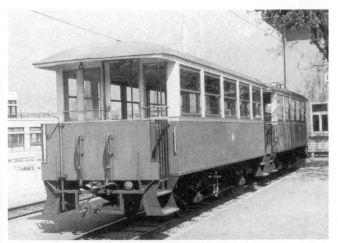

It was during the early 'seventies that the first real threat to the existence of trams materialised with the publication of plans for a new Autobahn through the Inn valley. These confirmed that the new road would cut through both mountain lines and most of the Bergisel depot complex. Pressure mounted from the authorities for the closure of the complete tramway system, but this was vigorously opposed by local interest groups, communities served by the trams and the public in general. With the support of the Institute of Transport and Tourism they were able to persuade the Transport Ministry to re-route the Autobahn further to the south, and thus lifted the threat to the trams.

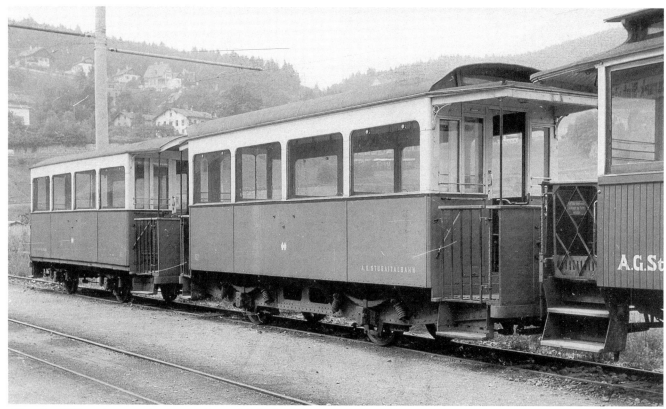

After the STJ motor cars had proved unsuitable for passenger operation, the two refurbished trailers, 161 and 162, were transferred to the Stb where they were in use until 1967. This early 1960s photograph captured both of them in the siding at Stubaitalbahnhof. *(collection Mackinger)*

Maria-Theresien-Strasse is the location for this interesting scene, showing Hall bogie car 5 waiting on the centre track before taking-up an extra duty to Hall, while sister car 1 prepares to depart a regular service on the same route. On the left, route A trolleybus 26 has just pulled-up at the stop, 01-05-72. *(W.Kreutz)*

The IVB, which had been contemplating the depot's replacement because of its incompatibility with the needs of a modern tramway, purchased a piece of land adjacent to the Stubaitalbahnhof, and digging of the foundations for a combined tram and bus depot began early in 1974. The layover track outside the Stubaitalbahnhof was lifted, and a single-track ramp installed to provide direct access for the Stb cars to the depot concourse and Pastorstrasse, paving the way for the life long wish of the AGStb to run its trams into the city.

Route 4 closes

However, as part of the preparations for the 1976 Winter Olympic Games included major road reconstruction by Olympisches Dorf (Olympic Village), tram route 4 to Hall was forced to close and this occurred on 8 June 1974 after eighty-three years' service. Replacement bus route 4 took over on the

following day and the tracks were lifted beyond Hungerburgbahn for reuse on the Igls line.

The lower-powered Hall cars and several trailers were withdrawn and offered for sale: motor car 1 and trailer 138 went to the Tramway Museum in Graz, motor car 5 and trailer 135 were despatched to Eurotram Klagenfurt, motor cars 7-8 and trailers 119/22 went to the Autobahn service station at Gries am Brenner where the former were adapted for use as kiosks selling petrol coupons, and the trailers as *Hunde Restaurants* in which motorists could feed their dogs in safety. Later insolvency of the service station forced the sale of motor car 7 and the trailers to a guest house at Weer, and motor car 8 joined the *Österreichische Lokalbahngesellschaft* in Payerbach. Trailer 140 was sold to a private owner in Raitis, and sister cars 117/21/23/39 to the expanding Eurotram fleet at Klagenfurt where they were ideally suited for use on the museum's horse tramway.

7. Modernisation

Having decided to retain the tramway, the IVB began preparing for the system's modernisation, the first phase of which would see the replacement of the remaining 2-axle cars and bogie car 60. Phases two and three would comprise upgrading the Igls and Stubaital lines. The Board decided that the most cost-effective option was to purchase a number of second-hand articulated trams on offer from various German systems and refurbish them in its own workshops. Consequently, a batch of 6-axle double-ended cars was obtained from the city of Hagen, followed by an assortment of 6- and 8-axle single-ended cars from Bielefeld. Over a period of years, the centre body sections were switched from one type to another to produce a fleet to match the service requirement.

The Hagen cars

In 1976 the German city of Hagen was in the final stages of closing its tramway and disposing of its fleet of well maintained 6-axle (GT6) double-ended articulated cars. An IVB delegation was sent to inspect them and a contract for the purchase of eight cars was signed in June. Built in 1960 by Düwag and fitted with Kiepe electrical equipment they were numbered 62-9 in the Hagen fleet, and were delivered to Innsbruck by rail in August 1976. They were repainted in a revised livery of red and cream with grey waist band and renumbered 82-9, car 86 making the first of the type's test runs through the city streets on 13 October. Two months later, cars 86 and 87 entered service on route 1.

When the Hagen tramway system closed in 1976, the IVB purchased eight 6-axle articulated cars for service on the urban routes. Numbered 62-9 in their home city, the IVB renumbered them 82-9. These two depot views depict cream and green car 66 (above) shunting a sister car across Klostergasse shortly after being unloaded at Westbahnhof (W.Kreutz) and (below), looking very smart in their new livery, two Hagen cars, headed by 82, laying-over at the route 1 terminus.   (collection Mackinger)

The entry into service of the Hagen cars saw the withdrawal of the last 2-axle stock. Car 21, seen here at Berg Isel with a 140-series trailer, was rebuilt as the system's railgrinder in 1971 and still operates in that capacity. (collection Mackinger)

On 14 October, work began implementing a new one-way system to improve traffic flows in the central area of the city. This required the tracks in Maria-Theresien-Strasse, Burggraben, Museumstrasse, Brunecker Strasse and Salurner Strasse to be relaid to form a single-track clockwise loop. As a result of this change, late evening route 6 cars were cut-back to terminate at Bergisel.

In order to reduce running costs on the Stb, the ticket offices at Mutters, Kreith and Telfes were closed and the station masters' houses sold off. Thereafter, passengers were required to purchase their tickets from on-board conductors. Two-way radios were provided for communications between train crews and the line controller.

Meanwhile, construction of the new depot (Betriebshof Wilten) continued apace. Containing an integrated central workshop with full overhaul facilities, it would provide covered storage for up to 100 buses and 56 six-axle tramcars. Used as the press and television centre for the 1976 Winter Olympic Games, it was officially opened on 17 September 1977.

A final clearout of redundant cars occurred in the spring of 1978, with the despatch of motor cars 18/28/31/60 and trailer 144 to the Eurotram museum, and motor car 20 to the museum group in Graz, while sister car 19 and trailer 147 were reassigned as IVB museum cars.

As construction of the Inntal Autobahn progressed, new sections of permanent way, linked by a single-span viaduct, were installed to enable route 6 to continue in operation, but the need to replace the rolling stock used on the line became a high priority. To this end, GT6 car 89 was subjected to a series of tests over the route and, although these proved satisfactory the passenger capacity of the Hagen cars was deemed too low, and the Hall cars given a reprieve.

75 years of the Stubaitalbahn

The 75th anniversary of the Stubaitalbahn was celebrated on 7 September 1979 with decorated trains and *Festen*, but of more importance was an announcement from the AGStb that it was proposing to convert the line to dc supply and operation using more modern rolling stock. To check for adequate clearances in the tunnels, a test run was made over the line as far as Sonnenburgerhof four days later using car 84 drawing power supplied via a temporary 600-volt dc feeder from the Stb depot. In the late evening of 12 September 1980, car 85 reached Kreith using a similar connection. The conversion could not proceed, however, until a double-ended car with sufficient capacity became available.

The Bielefeld system sold fifteen articulated trams to the IVB in the early 'eighties and the first car, ex-812, made a round-trip to Hungerburgbahn on 28-08-80, still in its orange and white livery. It is seen here in Ing.-Etzel-Strasse on the return leg. (W.Kreutz)

Three splendid views of the Stubaitalbahn during the final years of ac operation. (top) The Patscherkopfel mountain and Stubai valley provide a stunning backdrop for this three-car train as it approaches Luimes on a Fulpmes-bound service. (G. Breitfuss) (centre) The driver of motor car 2 brings his Innsbruck-bound train to a halt at Mutters station. Although double-heading was quite common, the pantograph on the second motor car has been lowered, possibly because most of the return journey is downhill. (collection Mackinger) (below) The Stubaitalbahn crews have always been a friendly bunch and like nothing more than to share the view from the front with their passengers. This tranquil setting shows a four-car train headed by motor car 4 passing Raitis en-route for Fulpmes. (G. Breitfuss)

Before entering service, the centre body sections were removed from the 8-axle Bielefeld cars for transfer to the Hagen cars. The two outer section were reformed into a 6-axle unit as depicted here with car 32 at the Amras terminus of route 3 in 1982. The car behind is operating a peak-hour only 3/1 service to Berg Isel. (collection Mackinger)

Cars from Bielefeld

At the turn of the decade, Bielefeld began to replace its first-generation articulated cars with Stadtbahn cars, and disposing of its fleet of single-ended 6-axle (GT6) and 8-axle (GT8) Düwag cars of 1957/62-3 vintage. In 1980, the IVB purchased one GT6 (825) and two GT8 (812/4) cars. As the Igls line had a stub-end terminus and could only be operated by double-ended cars, the centre section was removed from car 812 and transferred to Hagen car 87 to produce a car of adequate capacity for operation on the line. Both it and Hagen GT6 cars 85/9 received modifications for operation on the steeply-graded inclines. A new timetable was prepared requiring one car during off-peak and two at peak times. Car 87 would be permanently rostered on the route, leaving the second car to be drawn from the other two.

The two halves of Bielefeld 812 were joined together to produce a GT6 car, and following an overhaul and repaint in the Innsbruck livery it entered service on route 1 on 25 March 1981 as number 31. A second car, number 814, received similar treatment and entered service as

car 32 in April; its centre section being transferred to Hagen car 83 which was also modified for use on route 6.

Final bow for Hall tram sets

The final scheduled passenger service of a Hall tram set took place during the afternoon of 19 February 1981, when bogie car 3, bedecked with flowers, bunting and pennants, hauled four 2-axle trailers through the snow capped woods to Igls, closely followed by car 87, bringing an end to trailer operation by the IVB. Bogie cars 2-4 were initially retained as works cars and were subsequently introduced on more lucrative private-hire and tourist services. The body from car 6 was sold to the *Österreichische Lokalbahngesellschaft* at Payerbach in 1981 and its bogies retained for spares.

On 12 October 1981, the old Bergisel depot was closed and, following the transfer of serviceable equipment, tools and rolling stock to Wilten depot, the buildings were demolished to make way for commercial development. Part of the site was transformed into an attractive tram terminus for route 1, with flower beds, shrubs and passenger facilities.

Two popular locations for photographers on route 6 are Tantegert station and loop, and the bridge over the river Sill. (left) At the former, motor car 3 brings an Igls-bound train into the station while a down-train prepares to depart for Innsbruck in the 1970s. (right) Crossing the old Sillbrücke is a three-car Igls train made-up of motor car 2 and trailers 102 and 101. The bridge was later demolished as autobahn construction progressed and replaced by a modern concrete structure, 15-05-67. (collection Mackinger)

(above) Late 1980 at Bergisel and Hagen car 85 is about to depart on a special duty over route 6 prior to the withdrawal of the veteran tram sets, one of which is standing on the right headed by motor car 3.
(collection Mackinger)

(right) Adorned with garlands and "Letzte Fahrt" placards, Hall car 3 waits to haul the last scheduled motor/trailer set up to Igls, 19-02-81.
(W.Kreutz)

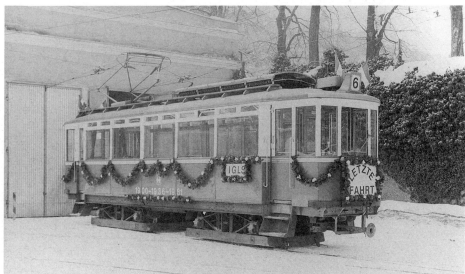

Environmental awareness

As smog clouds began to intermittently form over the cities, and more detailed information on the damage being caused through pollution to the nation's forests became public, increasing attention was focused on the major culprit – the combustion engine. To demonstrate its commitment to reducing the levels of exhaust emissions, the government offered financial inducements to persuade transport undertakings to increase their use of electrically-powered vehicles. The IVB responded by conducting a feasibility study into the introduction of a tram route to Olympisches Dorf. Plans for a line running from Maria-Theresien-Strasse through Pradl and Reichenau, operated by more second-hand trams from Bielefeld, were published in January 1982, and six 8-axle cars were obtained in July and August in anticipation. In the workshops, preparation of the Bielefeld cars was accelerated enabling GT6 car 33 (ex-825) to enter service in August 1982, and 34 (ex-811) in February 1983 following the removal of the latter's centre section. Hall bogie car 4 was declared surplus to requirements and placed in store.

The Council, however, could not agree as to whether trams or trolleybuses should be introduced on the Olympisches Dorf route, and the debate dragged on for

three more years. Ultimately, the decision was taken to build two trolleybus routes, based on the lower installation costs incurred.

New life for the Stubaitalbahn

Work now began transferring the centre sections from six Bielefeld cars to the remaining 6-axle Hagen cars in preparation for their use on the Stubaitalbahn. Staff training began in March 1982 on the Igls line and the changeover from ac to dc was scheduled for the autumn of 1983. Power would be supplied from a new 850-volt dc installation via transformers and rectifiers in Wilten depot, Kreith and Telfes.

As if in protest at its impending demise, a mysterious incident occurred on the Stb on 7 May 1982 when unmanned motor car 3 started up from the depot and accelerated across the depot yard before crashing into the station building, sustaining substantial damage in the process. It was stripped of usable equipment and the body scrapped. In the same year, a new halt called Birchfeld was opened at the Götzener Strasse crossing to serve the expanding eastern fringe of Mutters. Work on the Stb's conversion to dc operation progressed at a rapid pace, and passenger services were suspended on the afternoon of 13 January 1983 to allow cars 83 and 86

Bergisel depot was closed in October 1981 and a new landscaped terminus for tram routes 1 and 6 constructed on the site. A 6-axle Hagen lays-over on the left while passengers heading for Igls patiently queue to pay the conductor on 8-axle Hagen car 83.
(collection Mackinger)

to make trial runs to Fulpmes and back. As no serious problems were encountered, a full test programme was initiated and the decision taken to bring the changeover forward to 23 June 1983, on the basis that sufficient 8-axle Hagen cars would be available by then.

The day dawned warm and sunny and hundreds of people turned out to say farewell to their faithful servants. The last ac-powered train, comprising decorated motor cars 1 and 2, passenger trailers 13, 14, 16 and 17 and goods trailer 22, departed from Stubaitalbahnhof at 17:20. It took three hours to cover the 18 kilometres, having been forced to make lengthy stops for the benefit of the enthusiastic crowds encountered along the way. A huge canon mounted on wagon 22 was fired at each stop in final salute. When the train returned to Stubaitalbahnhof, the line was closed to allow essential alterations to be completed; a temporary bus service being operated between Bergisel, Natters, Mutters and Kreith.

The withdrawn ac rolling stock was stored in the Stubaitalbahn depot in the hope that at least a few cars might be preserved, and this encouraged a group of enthusiasts to form the Tiroler MuseumsBahnen (TMB) museum society. Within a year it had taken over the responsibility for the station and depot buildings and the entire withdrawn Stb fleet, none of which was scrapped.

dc operation

The inaugural runs on the reconstructed line took place on the 2 July 1983 using decorated Hagen GT8 cars (82/3/6) in convoy and several thousand people turned out to witness this new era. Until car 85 was returned to service with a new centre section at the end of the month, some duties were operated by 6-axle cars 84/8/9. The opportunity was also taken to renumber car 89 to 81 to realign the fleet numbers of the Hagen cars within the IVB convention. With a power supply now compatible with that of the urban tramway, the life-long ambition of the AGStb to penetrate into the city was fulfilled as its services were

On the afternoon of 13 January 1983, the Stubaitalbahn was closed to normal service to permit Hagen cars 83 and 86 to make test runs to Fulpmes and back using a temporary dc supply. The cars are seen here coasting down the section between Telfes and Fulpmes on the outward run. *(W.Kreutz)*

Hundreds of people turned out on 23 June, 1983, to witness the withdrawal of the ac cars and the end of an era. Comprising motor cars 2 and 1 and with trailers 13, 14, 17, and 16 in tow, the last train (above) is ready to depart from Stubaitalbahnhof on the final service. Bringing-up the rear, open goods-wagon 22 carried a huge canon which was fired as the train stopped at each station along the line. At Hölltal. (right), the penultimate service, operated by motor car 4 and trailers 12 and 15, passes the last train and continues on its way down to Innsbruck.
(G. Breitfuss)

extended over route 1's tracks to Hauptbahnhof from the same day. In addition, a more frequent, regular and faster service was offered, with trams departing Hauptbahnhof at 75-minute intervals.

In an experiment aimed at attracting more tourists to the line, the AGStb introduced special *Nostalgiefahrten* (nostalgic trips) running from Hauptbahnhof to Fulpmes using vintage Hall and IMB rolling stock. The first run occurred on 7 September 1983 and proved so popular that the trips were integrated into subsequent summer Wednesday schedules. A small band plays traditional Austrian music in the rear trailer for the entertainment of passengers.

Following the installation of a passing-loop at Telfeser Wiesen, the headway on the Stb was reduced to 50-minutes from 27 May 1984. From the same date, three additional evening workings were introduced

between Hauptbahnhof and Mutters, but through working to Fulpmes still ceased after 20:00. On 1 August, another new halt called Burgstall was opened on the northern fringe of Mutters to serve the growing number of commuters and a supermarket.

Upgrading the Igls line

Attention then turned to the final phase of the transformation of the Igls line and its extension into the city. A third batch of trams, comprising two GT8 and four GT6 cars, was purchased from Bielefeld towards the end of 1983, and upgrading of the infrastructure for operation with these cars began in the following year. Because these were single-ended vehicles with doors on one side only, a second platform was installed at each halt and the stub-end terminus at Igls lifted and replaced by a reversing loop. To cater for people visiting the nearby castle and cemetery, a new halt was built at Schloss

Similar scenes to those on the previous page were repeated for the inaugural trip under dc power on 2 July, 1983. Three garlanded Hagen 8-axle cars, 82, 83 and 86, carried guests from Stubaitalbahnhof to Fulpmes and back, making long stops to give local inhabitants the opportunity to savour the 'new' rolling stock. (left) A makeshift ceremonial ribbon has been strung across the front of the leading car at Telfes prior to the convoy's departure for Fulpmes (below), where another large crowd awaits further ceremony and speeches.
(G. Breitfuss)

Ambras. In 1985, Bielefeld GT8 car 801 was brought out of store, overhauled, repainted and renumbered 51 to begin a new series for single-ended 8-axle cars. As the work on the line was still in progress, it entered service on route 1 in April 1985 where it was joined by sister car 52 (ex-803) and two more Bielefeld GT6 cars 38/9 (ex-805/40) in the following year. These were also fitted with the modifications needed for use on the Igls line.

The changeover took place on 31 May 1987, and route 6 was extended over the tracks of route 1 to Hungerburgbahn from the same day, running on a schedule requiring two Bielefeld cars on rotation from route 1. Hagen car 87 was transferred to the Stb. The routine was in operation until January 1997, and worked as follows:

Outbound

The tram departing from Hungerburgbahn at 4 minutes past each hour displayed route 6 – Igls. On arrival at Bergisel, it would wait for the inbound car to arrive from Igls and then continue its upward journey.

Inbound

Cars departed from Igls at 5 minutes past the hour, and on arrival at Schloss Ambras the driver changes the blinds to show route 1 – Hungerburgbahn.

Because of the timing of the rotation, the modified cars could not always be positioned at the Hungerburgbahn terminus for the 4-minutes past the hour departure, so another four Bielefeld GT6 cars were modified for operation on route 6. This included car 802 which was taken out of store and overhauled before entering service as car 41 on 14 July 1987.

One-man operation

The IVB decided that to reduce its expanding wage bill it had to dispense with conductors, and the conversion to one-man operation commenced with car 33 in 1988. Route 3 became fully one-man operated in April 1989 and, with the exception of the Stb, the conversion was completed in 1993.

On the Stb a new halt, called Brandeck, was opened midway between Kreith and Telfeser Wiesen on 31 May 1987, its main purpose being to provide an alighting/boarding point for walkers using the adjacent footpath

Modernisation on the Stb

Although the Hagen cars were rugged and reliable vehicles they were by now nearly thirty years old. So the AGStb decided to modernise these and contracted Rotax of Wien to refurbish the complete batch at a cost of ATS 32 million; approximately £200 000 per car at 1990 exchange rates. This may seem a large amount of money to spend on 30-year old trams, but, when their anticipated 50-year lifespan was compared with the £1.2 million it would have cost for one new tram, refurbishment was considered the most appropriate option. The first car was dispatched by rail in August 1989 and the programme was completed three years later.

Fresh out of the paintshop, Bielefeld car 51 (above) poses for the camera alongside the administration block at Wilten depot in 1985. One of only three 8-axle cars of the type operated by the IVB, it was used initially on route 1 while a turning loop was installed at the Igls terminus of route 6. (collection Mackinger)

(right) During the conversion to one-man operation, driver-only cars were identified by broad blue bands with the word "Schaffnerlos" in white. Car 38, which was one of six 6-axle cars modified for use on route 6, was displaying the bands when photographed in Egger-Lienz-Strasse, 09-95. (author)

These two photographs illustrate the progressive modernisation of the Hagen cars. (above) In 6-axle form, car 89 is very much in as-purchased condition and was caught during a layover at Bergisel in 1981 when operating on route 6.
(collection Mackinger)

Sixteen years later, the same car is seen at Fulpmes (right), having been fitted with a Bielefeld centre section in 1984, when it was also renumbered 81, and revised headlighting and tinted windscreens fitted during refurbishment in 1991.
(author)

The refurbishment programme was funded from a ATS 52 million state grant, provided for modernisation of the line during the period 1991 to 1995. Other proposed improvements included

- the introduction of a 35-minute headway.
- automated ticketing to replace conductors – completed in 1998.
- the installation of a passing loop at Luimes – completed in 1994.
- further improvements to the trams.
- redecoration and improvements to stations – completed in 1995.
- reappraisal of the earlier proposal for the *Sellraintalbahn* branch line from Birchfeld (Mutters) to Grinzens (via Götzens, Birgitz and Axams).

In October 1989, bogie cars 61-6 were withdrawn as they could no longer handle the high number of passengers using the trams, especially during peak-hours. Car 62 which had sustained damage following a derailment was stripped of serviceable equipment and scrapped, and car 61 presented to the TMB museum group. To make up the shortfall, Bielefeld GT6 car 823 was taken out of store and prepared for service using equipment removed from Bielefeld GT6 car 837, which had been purchased to provide a source of spares. It entered service in November 1990 as car 42.

Traffic management

By the late 1980s, Innsbruck was suffering from chronic traffic congestion and unacceptably high levels of pollution. Surveys had confirmed that a record number of cars were entering the city, and environmental groups organised a series of demonstrations aimed at paralysing the main arterial routes. This stunned the Council into commissioning three acknowledged authorities in transport planning, Professors Retzko from Darmstadt, and Kirchhoff and Stracke from München, to produce a traffic management strategy for the Innsbruck conurbation. In their report, entitled *Verkehrswissenschaftliche Konzept (VKZ)*, published in May 1989, they outlined several options which would make dramatic improvements to the quality of life in the city. These included:

Short term

- Deter motorists from bringing their cars into the city by closing off or restricting access to specific major through roads.
- Limit access to the central thoroughfares to pedestrians, cyclists and public transport vehicles only.
- Reduce the number of inner-area car parking spaces and increase charges for those remaining.
- Upgrade and expand the tram and trolleybus network.
- Install Park & Ride (P & R) facilities close to the three Autobahn exits, and provide direct and frequent public transport services from these to the city centre.

The proposals for the second-generation trolleybus network are covered in a later chapter. The proposals for the tramway were modest and comprised;

- An extension of route 3 from its current terminus into Amras village.

- A new route (numbered 2) linking the proposed P & R facility by the Olympic swimming pool to the central area loop, running via Anton-Eder-Strasse and Amraser Strasse with a possible extension to the Kongresszentrum.
- An extension of route 1 from Bergisel to the proposed Olympic pool P & R.

Long term

- Westward extension of new route 2 along Innrain to Wiltenberg.
- Westward extension of route 3 along Innrain to Höttinger Au.
- Further eastward extension of route 3 to the shopping centre and P & R at Bleiche.
- Construction of a new tram route 4 running from Hötting West and via Innrain and Museumstrasse to Olympisches Dorf and Hall.
- Conversion of bus routes A, B and C to trolleybus operation.

The Council indicated its acceptance of most of the report by closing several roads and converting others for one-way working.

Increasing complaints from passengers on route 6 highlighted overcrowding on the smaller GT6 cars, particularly during rush-hours, as a major factor for the dwindling patronage on this route. As the rotation of trams between routes 1 and 6 made it impossible to assign one of the two GT8 cars on every route 6 duty, the decision was taken to introduce more single-ended 8-axle cars. To achieve this, the centre section from Bielefeld car 809 was purchased in 1991 and inserted between the front and rear sections of car 32 to form new GT8 car 53. The intention was to convert car 31 to GT8 car 54, but a suitable centre section has never materialised.

When the Lohner-built bogie cars were overhauled in the early 'eighties the white window surrounds were repainted cream, a grey waist band added and the pronounced 'V' under the windscreen painted over. Car 64 exemplifies this condition as it turns from Salurner Strasse into Maria-Theresien-Strasse, 06-84. (author)

Having completed the climb up from Innsbruck, Bielefeld 8-axle car 53 accelerates away from the Lans-Sistrans halt on the relatively flat section towards Igls in September 1995. This car entered service with the IVB as 6-axle car 32 in 1982 and was converted to 8-axle configuration in 1991 following the acquisition of a centre section from Bielefeld. (author)

The Marktplatz stop was built on a former car park in Innrain and opened in December 1995 to provide interchange facilities between tram, trolleybus and motorbus services. Equipped with digital information displays, passenger shelters and a confectionary kiosk, it is now one of the main hubs on the system. Here, car 41 turns into Bürgerstrasse under traffic light control. (collection Mackinger)

8. The centenary of Innsbruck Trams

To celebrate the centenary of the tramway, the IVB and TMB organised a series of special events. The first of these took place on 1 June 1991 when Hall bogie car 2 hauled two Igls trailers and restored Hall open trailer car 16 over the surviving section of the original steam-operated route, between Maria-Theresien-Strasse and Hungerburgbahn, followed by a run to Igls.

The parade

The major event of the year was a parade of historic trams through the city on 7 September. Both the IVB staff and TMB members spent months preparing the veteran cars, with priority being given to the 1942 Breda-built bogie car 60 which had recently returned to the city after years out of use at Eurotram. Another returned exile was LBIHiT 2-axle trailer 143 from the tramway museum group in Graz. Work on restoring Igls trailer 105 to 1900 condition had been in progress for a year, and was finished in the attractive dark green IMB livery complete with authentic coat of arms. Last of the preserved trams was former IVB bogie car 61 which had only been out of service for two years.

Tw 2 + Bw 105 and 16
Tw 3 + Bw 103 and 112
Tw 19 + Bw 147
Tw 61

To provide more space for the growing collection of preserved cars now housed in Wilten depot, withdrawn bogie cars 63/5 and Bielefeld GT6 car 824 were stripped of valuable parts and their bodies sold for scrap in 1992. Car 66 was similarly disposed of early in the following year and car 64 was dispatched to Eurotram.

During the summer of 1993 further parking restrictions and diversions were introduced in the central area, and yellow lines painted along Bürgerstrasse and Andreas-Hofer-Strasse segregated the trams from other road traffic. Work also began on the installation of a double-track tramway and wiring for bi-directional trolleybus operation along Museumstrasse, Burggraben, Marktgraben and Innrain, where a tram/trolleybus/bus interchange was built, and along Bürgerstrasse to the junction at Anichstrasse. The new section was ceremonially opened on 1 December 1995 using GT8

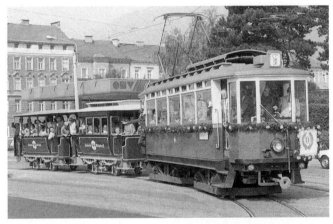 

A few of the cars that ran on the centenary parade are seen here at the Egger-Lienz-Strasse/Fritz-Konzert-Strasse junction, 07-09-91. Decorated Hall motor car 2 with restored trailers 105 and 16 in tow (left), proudly displays '100' on its dash, while bogie car 60 (right) negotiates the sharp curve on what was its first run under is own power since 1978. (collection Mackinger)

Saturday the seventh was a gloriously sunny day, and afforded the thousands of people who turned out to witness this historic event a day to remember. The route used was from Wilten depot via route 1 to Maria-Theresien-Strasse and Museumstrasse, round the Hauptbahnhof loop and via Anichstrasse, back to the depot. The streets in the central area were closed for two hours and tram route 1 suspended for the duration of the parade. The participating tramcars are listed below:

Tw 2 + Gw 204 and 262
Tw 84 as route Stb
Tw 88 as route 3/1
Tw 52 as route 6
Tw 60 as route 1/3
Tw 61 as TMB
Tw 19 + Bw 147
FKB5366 (petrol) + Bw 143
Atw 21 Railgrinder
Atw 200 Snowbroom
Tw 3 + Bw 102, 103, 106 and 112 as route 4
Tw 2 (second time round) + Bw 105 and 16

(Note: Tw = motor car, Bw = trailer car, Gw = goods wagon, Atw = works car)

In the afternoon, the following preserved trams operated as direct replacements for service cars on routes 1 and 3:

car 52 and a Hall tram set comprising bogie car 3 and trailers 16/105. Tram routes 1 and 6 were diverted to run over the new section, leaving route 3 to serve the Hauptbahnhof, Salurner Strasse, Maria-Theresien-Strasse loop. Inbound Stb trams were diverted over the new section operating a clockwise-loop via Innrain, Marktgraben, Burggraben and Museumstrasse to Hauptbahnhof, and returning via Salurner Strasse and Anichstrasse as before. The closure to vehicular traffic of this major artery had the desired effect, and passenger loadings on the IVB services soon began to rise.

The unused track on the south side of Anichstrasse was disconnected and parts of it asphalted over; which is a pity as it would provide a diversionary route should the new alignment become blocked at any time.

A crash on the Stubaitalbahn!

At 12.25 on 22 April 1995, a head-on collision occurred between cars 82 and 87 as they negotiated a blind bend, 200 metres north of Mutters station. Car 82 had passed the regular Fulpmes bound tram as scheduled at Telfes Wiesen, and continued on to Mutters where it should have waited for the Saturday-only school service to arrive from Innsbruck. Instead, it continued on its way with the inevitable result. As the line is operated using line-of-sight regulations, there are no signals to prevent such accidents. Both drivers and thirteen passengers were injured and severe damage was sustained by both trams.

The undamaged section from car 82 was exchanged with the damaged section on 87, allowing a reformed car 87 to re-enter service on 13 May. The damaged sections were stripped of useful equipment and scrapped while the undamaged centre section from car 82 was placed in store. A replacement 6-axle car was purchased from Bochum in Germany and fitted with the salvaged centre section to form a new car 82 which entered service in April 1998.

To ensure similar incidents could not recur, drivers were instructed to obtain radio clearance from the Control Centre before entering a single-track section. A progress sheet, attached to the control panel, was used by the driver to record how far he could proceed before the next check-in, and which other cars would be encountered at each passing loop.

The scene of devastation that faced rescue teams on 22 April 1995, following the head-on crash between cars 82, seen here, and 87 on a sharp bend north of Mutters. The damaged sections from both cars were scrapped and a replacement car purchased from Bochum. (W.Kreutz)

In April 1995 a new halt called Feldeler was opened between Raitis and Ausserkreith, to serve a new housing complex, and a passing loop added in the following January.

VerkehrsVerbund Tirol

In 1987 agreement in principle was reached between the IVB, ÖBB, PTT and private bus companies, within the province of Tirol, for the introduction of a fully-integrated regional fare system designed to attract more people on to the abundant public transport services in the region. The publication of a proposal for a common fare structure for the Province Tirol occurred in 1988. Seven years later, on 1 April 1995, the VerkehrsVerbund Tirol (VVT), the largest of its kind in Austria, was born. Instead of buying a ticket for each stage of a journey that might involve several changes, passengers can now complete the same journey with the purchase of a solitary ticket. A passenger beginning a journey in the country on a PTT bus, for example, could change to an ÖBB train and complete their journey to a suburb of Innsbruck using a combination of tram, trolleybus, IVB or private bus – with one ticket.

The end of the line for route 6?

Despite all these improvements, patronage on tram route 6 continued to decline. Early in 1996 the IVB announced that it could no longer afford to finance the ATS 3-4 million annual deficit, and that the line would be closed down on 31 October — unless an external source of finance was forthcoming. Frantic efforts were made to attract such funding, while international support for the line's retention, based mainly on its touristic value, poured in. Within days of the intended closure date the IVB announced a three-year reprieve as it had received offers of financial support from: the City Council, to the value of ATS 1.6 million; the *Land* Tirol for ATS 800 000; and Innsbruck Tourist Office for ATS 200 000. Further good news followed in October 1999 when the IVB announced that passenger loadings had increased over the duration of the reprieve, and that tram services to Igls would continue at least until the next review in October 2002, therefore enabling the centenary celebrations of the opening of the line on 27 June 2000 to proceed as planned.

Further reductions in the IVB's spiralling operating costs and growing deficit were achieved by extending the headways on routes 1 and 3 from 6- to 7½ minutes from 15 January 1997. This reduced the operational requirement for trams, allowing Lohner cars 74/7 to be placed in store and twenty three buses to be withdrawn for disposal. Car 39 was decorated to promote the benefits of using the IVB services. From the same date the timetable for route 6 was revised to operate every 90-minutes between 08:25 and 16:45 in the winter, and 08:00 to 19:45 in the summer, and the lower terminus was cut-back to Bergisel in the winter.

A newly-appointed Direktor, Herr Baltes, took a more ambitious approach, however, and reintroduced the 60-minute schedule on 26 June 1997 with trams departing Hauptbahnhof on the hour. To attract more tourists, the daily 10:00, 12:00 and 14:00 departures were assigned to a vintage Igls tram-set comprising a motor car, two trailers and a former Stb baggage car adapted for carrying up to ten bicycles. This facility was extended to the GT cars operating on the service, when four offside seats were removed to make way for a rail and securing straps on cars 52-3. The latter car was painted in a blue/silver livery to promote the service, which has seen an encouraging increase in the number of passengers, but its long-term future is still in the balance.

One-man operation on the Stubaitalbahn

The year 1997 proved to be an eventful year on the Stb. In the spring, the services of conductors were dispensed with following the installation of automatic ticket machines at the main stops, their desks being removed from the trams during their next major

One of the measures adopted to attract more passengers to route 6 was to repaint car 53 sky blue and adorn it with images portraying the main features of the line. The replacement of two rear seats with a rail for attaching bicycles has proved popular with mountain bikers. Here, the car awaits the inbound service from Igls to pass, Bergisel, 09-97. (author)

inspection. Tickets for single journeys could still be purchased from drivers, but multiple-ride tickets could only be bought at the IVB head office, the IVB kiosk at Marktplatz, the IVB Information Centre and the Mutters, Igls and Innsbruck tourist offices.

The ongoing programme of safety improvements on the Stb continued with the implementation of a new vehicle identification and location system. Induction coils installed at the ends of each passing loop and at other strategic locations, would receive signals from transponders fitted under the trams, and transmit the information to the Control Centre computer.

Amalgamation

In 1997, both the IVB and AGStb were incorporated with the region's electricity, gas and water holding company to form the Innsbrucker Kommunalbetriebe, which resulted in a subtle change to the latter's title; Stubaitalbahn GmbH.

Car 83 crosses from Marktgraben to Burggraben, passed the Tourist Information Centre on the left, on a quiet Sunday afternoon in September 1997. Note the change of title from A.G. to GmbH. (author)

In May 1998, car 40 (above) was the first tram to be repainted all-white and the rest of the fleet is gradually receiving the new livery. It was photographed at Marktplatz in the following September. The first Hagen car in the white scheme, number 81 (right), is seen leaving Fulpmes for the city in September 1999. (author)

The future

The appointment of Herr Baltes as the new Direktor has brought a remarkable turnround in the fortunes of the IVB. The undertaking is undergoing a complete image change with the introduction of the new livery, new staff uniforms, electronic arrival and destination indicator displays, and an extensive flow of passenger information, available from a new IVB Information Centre located at Stainerstrasse 2 (off Marktgraben) or via the internet (www.ivb.com).

Looking ahead the implementation of proposed tram route 2 to the Olympic Pool is unlikely to proceed because of the high construction costs, continued opposition by the powerful pro-trolleybus faction and the successful reintroduction of trolleybuses. The route, be it tram or trolleybus, will run as per the *Verkehrswissenschaftliche Konzept* recommendations from a new P & R facility by the pool, to the city centre, and via the tram route 3 clockwise loop back to the pool, operating as a shuttle service with limited stopping.

The extension of route 1 from Bergisel to the Olympic Pool P & R should, hopefully, get the go-ahead. This will require the doubling of the track for route 6 in Klostergasse and the construction of a new tramway in Wiesengasse.

These decisions will ultimately depend on the outcome of a study currently being carried out by the IVB in conjunction with consultants into the future of

transport in the city. The expectation is that a decision will be made in favour of the trams and that seventeen new cars will be needed on the urban system and six on the Stubaitalbahn.

That the Innsbruck trams survive is nothing short of a miracle and one can only hope that the positive attitude of the current administration continues, thus ensuring that local inhabitants and the thousands of visitors to the region, will continue to enjoy the delights of panoramic tramrides well into the new millennium.

This page illustrates the different types of trailer operated by the various companies in Innsbruck. (above, left) Car 16 was rebuilt from 3-window car 101ᴵᴵ in the late 1980s by the TMB to represent an LBIHiT open-sided summer car of 1892, and is seen at Igls in August 1992. (above, right) Owned and operated by the IVB on route 6, special occasions and Nostalgiefahrten, the twin arch-shaped windows on car 102 identify it as being a pre-war rebuild. Fulpmes, 09-91. (below, left) IVB car 103, built by Graz in 1900, retains the original body styling comprising a 4-window saloon and clerestory roof. Fulpmes, 09-91. (below, right) Taken a week before the centenary parade, car 105 was pictured in the IVB depot being prepared for the installation of its windows following a rebuild by TMB members to original 1900 condition and green livery   (all, author)

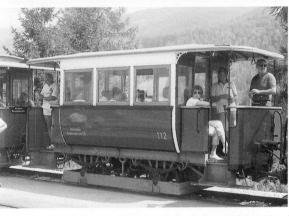

(above, left) Standing by the wheel turning machine in Wilten depot, car 111 is having final checks before joining the TMB operational fleet, 09-95. (above, right) Fitted with a new body in 1945 after suffering serious bomb damage, IVB car 112 displays the final design applied to these cars; a 3-bay saloon and flat roof with no clerestory. Fulpmes, 09-91. (below, left) Following withdrawal in 1973, car 143 went with several others to the Tramway Museum at Graz. It was retrieved by the TMB in 1990, and restored to operational condition, 09-95 (three, author). Possibly the sole-surviving centre-entrance trailer to operate in Innsbruck, former Basel car 160 waits outside the Klostergasse sheds for a turn on route 3, 26-05-64   (J.Wyse)

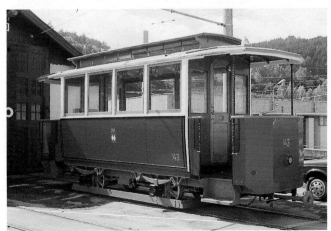
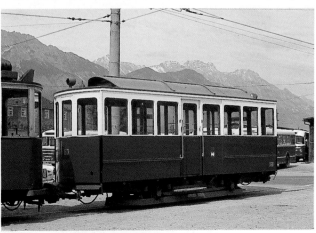

A variety of tramcars was operated by the IVB during the fifties and sixties. Nearing the end of its passenger carrying days, motor car 54 and trailer (above, left) approach the temporary terminal stub in Egger-Lienz-Strasse in July 1956. Following withdrawal, 54 was assigned to the works fleet where it survived for a further decade, before becoming an exhibit at the city's Zeughaus. In 1998 it was obtained by the TMB which plans to restore it, (F.Hunt). Another familiar site in the city were the Zürich motor cars and Merano trailers the last of which were withdrawn in 1978. Motor car 19 and trailer 147 (above, right) were retained and are a common site once again following restoration work by the museum society in the mid-1980s. (TMB)

The north end of Leopoldstrasse had a regular tram service until the end of 1964, and the single track section was a favourite spot for photographers. The Basel cars operated most duties on route 3 and one of them, motor car 26, is seen heading through the narrow section (above, left) towards Wiltener Platz, 26-05-64 (J.Wyse). Taken on the same day at the Museumstrasse/Brunecker Strasse junction, car 26 and 143 head east towards Pradl, (F.Hunt). Car 26 was scrapped in 1966, but the trailer was preserved and currently resides at the TMB depot.

Undoubtedly one of the most popular trams to operate in Innsbruck, bogie car 60 spent most of its working life on route 1 where it could make the most of its speed and acceleration on the long sections of straight track. Having entered service in the Belgrade green and white livery it was repainted red and silver after the war and is pictured here behind a Basel tram set in Maria-Theresien-Strasse, 07-56, (J.Wyse). Withdrawn in 1977, it went to the Eurotram line in Klagenfurt as a static exhibit, before being retrieved for restoration by the TMB in 1990.

Preparation of the Bielefeld trams for service in Innsbruck lasted nearly a decade and as a consequence many of them stood idle in Wilten depot for some years. In these two views, refurbished Hall car 3 is sandwiched between car 803 and 840 (above, left) which became 52 and 39 respectively in the IVB fleet, while bogie cars 64 and 66 await their next duties. (above, right) Car 823 was one of the oldest Bielefeld cars. Built in 1957 and purchased by the IVB in 1983, it finally entered service as 42 in 1990, 06-84

(both, author)

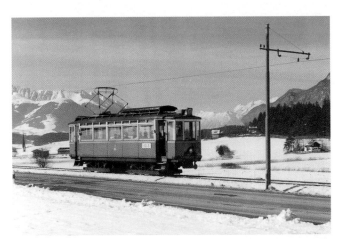

The winter snow brings thousands of skiers to the region and, as the tramway is often the only means of transportation during heavy falls, it has the task of taking them up to the slopes. Hall car 2 (above, left) has left Lanser See behind and is heading for Igls on a route 6 service on a crystal clear day. (above, right) In Maria-Theresien-Strasse, car 35 slides to a halt during some of the severest snow falls the city had experienced. Even the normally clear roadway has a thick covering, preventing the movement of rubber-tyred vehicles, 15-01-99

(D.Seifridsberger)

This picture-postcard scene was taken at Tantegert on route 6 and shows advertising car 51 arriving in knee-deep snow, the tracks having been kept clear by Snowbroom 200, 07-01-99

(D.Seifridsberger)

The line out to Hall was operated by steam-powered locomotives from 1891 until 1910 when faster electric bogie cars were introduced. A year later, it was integrated into the urban system as route 4 and ran in continuous service until closure due to road reconstruction in 1974. (top) A five-car set headed by car 1 is ready for departure from the Unteren Stadtplatz terminus in Hall, 26-05-64 (F.Hunt). (centre, left) The passing loop at Thaur with an off-peak three-car set headed by car 1 with trailers 123 and 124, en-route for Hall, 30-06-73 (M.Russell). (centre, right) The same location and motor car 7 has just arrived from Innsbruck while the set on the right is about to run alongside Haller Strasse towards Olympisches Dorf which can be seen under construction in the background (O. Knoll). (below) Route 4 was given a traditional send-off with decorated cars and period costume, the dubious honour of pulling the last tram bestowed on motor car 5. It is seen here at Thaur during one of its many stops on the return trip from Hall, 08-06-74.
(author's collection)

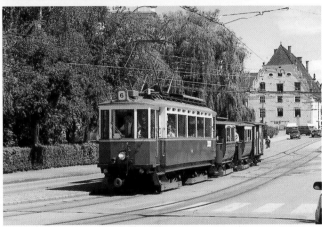

Hall cars 2 and 3 remain a familiar sight on the city's streets. (top) Car 2 was still in as delivered condition with twin bow collectors and matchboard bodywork when photographed at Berg Isel in July 1956, (F.Hunt), while twenty-four years later, the same car displays it's handsome rebuilt bodywork at Fulpmes (centre, left). Sister car 3 rumbles passed the IVB offices in Pastorstrasse (centre, right) on one of the special summer services on route 6, with two trailers and goods wagon 32, 09-98 (both, author). A decade of hard work by members of the TMB was rewarded in 1999 with the first appearance of this rake of four fully restored trailers (below), each representing a different period and operating company. Lined-up behind Hall car 3 at Bergisel are trailers 16, 105, 111 and 104, 01-08-99. (D.Seifridsberger)

Passengers enjoy the ride on the open platform of this Stb train as it coasts towards the Stubaital-bahnhof terminus, with trailer cars 14 and 12 bringing up the rear. Looking remarkably rural, the allotment area to the left is now part of Wilten depot, 24-05-64. (J.Wyse)

The procedure for turning trains at the Stb termini is illustrated in this scene at Stubaitalbahnhof. Motor car 4 shunts the trailers a short distance up the sloping mainline in the background. Having applied the brakes, the motor car is uncoupled and run back onto the siding on the right. The conductor then uses the handbrake to control the rake as it coasts under gravity into the station, enabling the motor car to be attached at the other end. The red and white trailer is STJ car 162, 27-05-64. (J.Wyse)

Motor car 4 was in very much as-built condition when photographed heading a train about to depart Stubaital-bahnhof for Fulpmes. It's bow collector is in the lowered position and the matchboard-style bodywork carries the brown and cream livery. Today, the station building is home for the TMB exhibition and book shop, 27-05-64. (F.Hunt)

During the mid-sixties, new bodies were built on the original underframes and trucks of the Stb trailers followed by limited modernisation of the motor cars. Single-arm pantographs replaced the bow collectors, steel dash panels were fitted in lieu of the matchboard-style originals and the IVB red and white livery superseded the rather dull brown and cream. This photograph of a train headed by motor car 4 was taken in 1973 and makes an interesting comparison with those on the previous page.
(M.Russell)

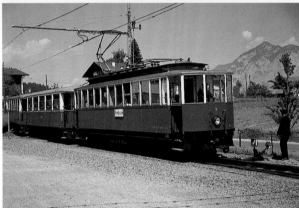

Nestling below the Nockspitze mountain, high above the Inn valley, the village of Mutters is a popular holiday resort and destination for tourists, many of whom make use of the Stb and it's picturesque little station. Pictured here in June 1975 are motor car 2 about to depart for Innsbruck (centre, left) and motor car 4 crossing Innsbruckerstrasse and into the station with a train from Fulpmes. Note that although power has been collected via pantographs for several years, the bows are still in situe on both cars.
(author)

A Stubaitalbahn train en-route from Telfeser Wiesen to Luimes in typical glorious scenery towards the end of ac operation on the line. Motor car 4 displays the final modifications made to these cars; twin headlights, removal of the bow collector and glazed doors to fully enclose the driver's cab.
(TMB)

When compared to their predecessors, the Lohner-built bogie cars had comparatively short lives due to their limited capacity, but were instrumental in securing the retention of the tram in Innsbruck. Car 65 runs passed the Wilten Basilica in Pastorstrasse (above) in the original red and white livery, 25-05-64. (centre, left) Car 66 displays its abundance of chrome trim as it prepares to turn from Museumstrasse into Egger-Lienz-Strasse, 25-05-64 (both, J.Wyse). The revised red and cream livery was applied to the batch in the early 'eighties as seen on car 61 (centre, right) as it turns from Falkstrasse in June 1984. This car is now preserved by the TMB.   (author)

The bogie cars were a common sight on route 1 until they were gradually ousted by the Bielefeld cars during the late 'eighties. Here, car 64 negotiates the curve leading from Fritz-Konzert-Strasse into Pastorstrasse in June 1984.   (author)

When cars 74/7 were stored in 1995, it looked like the beginning of the end for the Lohner-built 6-axle cars, but when drivers protested that they preferred them to the Düwag model, they were overhauled and returned to service. Recently overhauled car 71 received the white livery and returned to service on route 1, Museumstrasse, 09-99.
(author)

Looking very smart in a fresh coat of red and cream, car 76 takes the loop by-passing the Stb terminus in SüdTiroler Platz. The retention of most of the chrome trimmings on these cars enhances their appearance, 09-95.
(author)

Taken at the same location, this photograph shows car 77 after overhaul and repainting in the white livery. The single, fully-glazed front doorway, smaller saloon windows and single central headlight distinguishes the Lohner design from that of Düwag, 14-06-99.
(D.Seifridsberger)

Bergisel in June 1984 and Bielefeld car 36 turns into Klostergasse on a route 1 service bound for Hungerburgbahn. In the background, a route 1 bogie car lays-over on the loop while Hagen car 87 is ready to depart on a duty through the Patschberg forest to Igls. The Egger-Lienz-Strasse trambaan (centre, left) allows drivers to notch-up a reasonable turn of speed, being segregated from the traffic on either side. Car 37 seen here, decelerates on approaching the Fritz-Konzert-Strasse stop, 09-95. (centre, right) The same car accelerates away from Pastorstrasse en-route for Hungerburgbahn followed by car 53 inbound on route 6 from Igls. Although not officially withdrawn, car 37 has languished in the depot for nearly two years and may not re-enter service, 09-97. *(all, author)*

A busy scene at the Marktplatz interchange with recently overhauled Bielefeld car 41 on a route 1 service to Bergisel and trolleybus 820 heading for Olympisches Dorf on route O alongside a bus on route D, 09-99. *(author)*

The IVB had no advertising or pop-art colour schemes on its trams until a couple of years ago when the first appeared on a Bielefeld car. Since then several Bielefeld trams have adopted non-standard liveries and some of them are displayed on this page. (above, left) Car 31 on route 1 in Pastorstrasse is the "Culture" tram and bears images of the city's heritage around its bodywork, 09-98. The four lower quarter panels on advertising car 35 (above, right) are painted in different colours, Marktplatz, 09-99. Carrying advertisements over the white livery, car 39 is seen (below, left) at the new Sill Park stop in Amraser Strasse, 09-99 (three, author). It is unusual to see a 6-axle car on route 6 these days but perhaps on this occasion the IVB was taking its message to the mountains, car 39 at Bergisel (below, right), 04-12-99. (D.Seifridsberger)

A green skirt has been added to the white livery on advertising car 40 which is seen (above, left) on route 1 at Marktplatz, 09-99 (author). The more subtle message displayed on car 40 the year before is apparent in this view (above, right) taken at the route 3 terminus at Amras, 02-06-98 (D.Seifridsberger). All three 8-axle cars have appeared in different colours and two are depicted here. (below, left) Giving prominence to a city department store is car 51, waiting to depart Bergisel for Igls, 09-98. Seen at the same stop in the previous year (below, right), "Tourist" tram 53, the car that initiated the change from red and cream, 09-97. (both, author)

The cost of purchasing the eight, 6-axle cars from the city of Hagen in 1976 has been repaid many times over. Bought initially to replace the Zürich 2-axle stock on route 1, they were utilised as replacements for the Hall motor cars on route 6 in 1981 and finally, in 1983 they ousted the vintage ac trains from the Stubaitalbahn. (above, left) Little did the author realise that when he took this photograph of Hagen car 68 in its home city in 1975, he would capture it again nine years later as IVB car 88. It was the last of the batch to be converted to 8-axle and is seen turning into Pastorstrasse (above, right) on route Stb to Fulpmes, 06-84. As replacement for the bogie car-hauled trains on route 6, car 87 was fitted with a centre section from a Bielefeld car. It operated solely on the line for six years and was photographed (centre, right) approaching Igls on roadside reservation, 06-84. (three, author)

Two stout bridges known as the Mutterer and Kreitherer Brücke were built to carry Stubaitalbahn trains across deep ravines, and car 82 rumbles its way across the former (centre, left) with an Innsbruck-bound service in June 1984. (below, left) The longevity and immaculate condition of the Hagen cars is due both to their rugged construction and high standards of engineering and maintenance employed by IVB staff at Wilten depot. Car 81 is seen here leaving Telfes for Fulpmes during its thirtieth year, 09-90 (both, author). A perfect setting on a perfect day as car 86 approaches Nockhofweg during the early years of dc operation on route Stb. (TMB)

On this page, a picture of each of the Hagen trams on route Stb taken after their refurbishment by Bombardier-Rotax. (above, left) Car 81 bears the white livery and was photographed by TMB member Dieter Seifridsberger departing Fulpmes for Innsbruck, 25-10-98. The newest tram in Innsbruck is car 82, seen here (above, right) approaching Burgstall on a Fulpmes service in September 1998. Built in 1968, it was purchased from Bochum-Gelsenkirchen in 1995 as a replacement for accident victim car 82 and fitted with the centre section salvaged from the wreckage. (below, left) "Fahrschulwagen", driver training cars, are a rarity on the Stubaitalbahn as crew turnover is extremely low. Car 83 was, however, caught on a training run in the wooded area between Raitis and Feldeler in September 1997. (below, right) The Nordkette mountain range provides the perfect background for car 84 on the passing loop at Kreith station, 09-98. (three, author)

Car 85 stands alongside 83 at the Telfeser Wiesen halt (above, left), one of two scheduled crossing points on the line, 09-97. Its situation at the confluence of the Stubai valley with the Brenner Pass, offers magnificent views and is a popular alighting point for walkers. The final section of the line (above, right) and car 86 negotiates a sharp curve near Tenniscamp while en-route for Innsbruck. The scattered chalets and farms of Telfes with it's prominent church spire provide the backdrop for this September 1995 view. The final two photographs show route Stb trams running on the city section of the line. (below, left) Car 87 speeds along the Egger-Lienz-Strasse trambaan with passengers heading for the mountains, 09-95. (below, right) The dash on car 88 displays the most recent livery change being applied to the red and cream cars; smaller fleet numbers under a grey IVB flash and the removal of the Stubaitalbahn name on Stb cars. The location is Marktplatz, 09-99. (all, author)

Built in the mid-thirties by Fiat for the Italian city of Livorno, trolleybus 16 was one of four requisitioned for service in Innsbruck during the Second World War. Rebuilt with new front body panelling it survived until 1972 when it was sold to become a rest room with a construction company. In this view, it is turning from Wilhelm-Greil-Strasse into Salurner Strasse while operating on route C, 13-07-68. (M.Taplin)

In their modernised form, the Livorno trolleys looked rather smart and their robust construction ensured a service life of thirty-five years. Number 17 is about to be passed by a Gräf & Stift bus as it prepares to pull away from the Bozner Platz stop on a route C duty to Wiltenberg. Another Livorno trolley can be seen running down Brixner Strasse in the distance, 06-08-66. (M.Russell)

A hot summer day and a traffic policeman waves route C trolleybus 18 across the bustling junction from Maria-Theresien-Strasse into Markt-graben to continue its journey to Wiltenberg. Still in as-built condition, the bodywork has lasted well and a passenger is taking full advantage of the drop-down window, 07-56. (J.Wyse)

This photograph of a Gräf & Stift trolleybus in original form with a trailer in tow, taken by Jack Wyse a year before the trolley was rebuilt, conveys the square lines of the original design. The pair have just turned from Meraner Strasse into Maria-Theresien-Strasse and are heading for Wiltenberg on a peak-hour route C service, 26-05-64.

The final modernisation on the first generation trolleybus system involved the complete rebuilding of the Gräf & Stift vehicles in the 1960s and this extended their working lives by several years. (above, left) Trolleybus 24 on route A heads south along Maria-Theresien-Strasse for Hauptbahnhof. Also off interest is the three-track layout in use by the trams at that time, 30-06-73 (M.Russell). Trolleybus 25 displays its new bodywork as it passes the Annasäule column on a route A duty to Hauptbahnhof, 26-05-64 (J.Wyse). A bustling scene at the Maria-Theresien-Strasse stop as trolleybus 25 operating on route A cautiously pulls away for the short run to Hauptbahnhof, 30-06-73.   *(M.Russell)*

Twelve years after the closure of the first system, trolleybuses were reintroduced to the streets of Innsbruck. Opened in stages, the current system comprises two cross-city routes operated by modern articulated vehicles. (above, left) Opened in 1995, the Rehgasse extension of route R and trolleybus 812 departs the terminus for the city, 09-97. (above, right) The Triumphpforte in September 1998 and trolleybus 805 on route R emerges from the archway through which the trams had passed many years earlier. (left) Trolleybus 815 was the first of its type to receive the white livery and was photographed in SüdTiroler Platz on a route R service to Rehgasse, 09-98. (below) Conveying what appears to be a road safety message, trolleybus 826 picks-up passengers at Marktplatz before heading west to Peerhofsiedlung on route O, 09-97. (all, author)

9. The introduction of trolleybuses (1943-76)

The history of the trolleybus in Innsbruck dates back to 1938 when replacement of trams on the routes to Pradl and Hall was under discussion, but nothing further occurred until 1941 when the IVB applied to the Transport Ministry for permission to introduce trolleybuses on motor bus routes. Given the strict regulations on the supply of raw materials for non-military purposes, it was a little surprising when authorisation was forthcoming for the conversion of three bus routes:

A: Hötting – City Centre – **Amras** (6.56 km).

B: Reichenau – City Centre – **Pradl** (6.42 km).

C: Wiltenberg – City Centre – **Arzl** (7.37 Km).

Authorisation was also forthcoming for the construction of a 6.7-km trolleybus route between the city centre and the western suburb of Lohbachsiedlung, not previously served by motor buses, but this was subsequently dropped. A piece of land was identified for the depot at Leipziger Platz, and power would be supplied from a rectifier at the Dr. Glatzstrasse/Amraser-See-Strasse junction. Brown Boveri (BBC) of Mannheim were contracted to construct the overhead wiring, and an order was placed with Henschel for eighteen trolleybuses with 9.04 meter Kässbohrer bodies, and accommodation for 45 passengers.

Work began erecting the overhead wiring in January 1942, and in a change of plan the IVB decided to locate the depot alongside that of the trams at Berg Isel. Constructed of wood it was completed in November 1943, and access was provided via a single pair of wires running from Hallenbad via Hunoldstrasse, Tivoli (where a reversing-triangle was installed to provide a short test line) and the Sillbrücke.

Second-hand vehicles

In the meantime the trolleybus order was cancelled, on the direction of the authorities, so that Henschel could concentrate on the production of military vehicles and the IVB informed that suitable vehicles would be requisitioned from Italian systems. The first five vehicles were selected from a batch of eight built in 1936 by Breda for Roma, were painted in the city's two-tone green livery and arrived in Innsbruck in November 1943. Renumbered 10-14 they could easily be distinguished from subsequent deliveries by their central driving positions and three-piece windscreens. A conductor's desk was located inside the rear double-door entrance, and passengers alighted through a double-doorway behind the front nearside wheel. Passenger capacity was 22 seated and 37 standing. Tractive-power was provided by a single 99-kW motor driving the rear axle via a cardan-shaft and differential gears. As there were no spares, trolley 14 was used as a source of parts.

A second batch delivered on 12 December comprised four vehicles from a series of 35 trolleys built by Fiat in 1935/6 for operation in Livorno. They were fitted with CGE electrical equipment and painted all-over green. Two 28.5-kW motors powered the rear axle via cardan-shafts and an ingenious differential-gear system that varied the drive from each motor according to the direction of vehicle turn. Double-doors were located at the front (exit) and rear (entrance), and accommodation was provided for 21 seated and 40 standing passengers. These were allocated fleet numbers 15-18, and trolley 18 became the source of spares.

Inauguration

Preparations for the start of operations were brought to an abrupt halt by the first air raid on 15 December 1943, and it was not until 8 April 1944 that trolleybuses were able to begin running on the first service; route C between Arzl and Wiltenberg on a 30-minute headway. A further raid on 13 June resulted in a direct hit on the trolleybus depot, causing minor damage to trolleys 13 and 15. To reduce the risk of further damage, the five remaining vehicles were dispersed to open fields near Amras and Arzl overnight. The bomb-damaged vehicles were repaired and repainted all-over cream with brown fenders, mudguards and trolleybooms.

Despite these setbacks, trolleybus services on route A to Hötting, high up in the northern suburbs, commenced on 26 June, with services departing from a temporary loop at Innrain. Trolleybuses 10-13 were assigned to this hilly route as these were equipped with more efficient braking systems. The headway on this route was also 30-minutes.

The conversion to trolleybus operation of bus route B between Universitätsstrasse and Dreiheiligenstrasse took place on 9 August 1944, the fleet having been expanded with the arrival of four trolleybuses from San Remo. These were also CGE equipped Fiats and were built in 1939, but had bodies built by Cansa. As the San Remo system did not open until 1942,

It will be a long time before the travel bureau reopens judging by the bomb-damage on this row of buildings in Boznerplatz. This scene, believed to have been taken in 1946, sees trolleybuses 10 and 16 about to depart to the suburbs with full loads. Because of the material shortage number 16 was painted in a cream and brown livery. (W.Kreutz)

three of the requisitioned vehicles were operated on the system in Firenze for a couple of years. Twin 55.8-kW motors supplied traction to the rear axle on a short-wheelbase chassis, and being built of lightweight materials they were able to outpace most other vehicles from a standing start. Seating was provided for 22 passengers with standing room for 29. Assigned fleet numbers 19-22 they retained their all blue livery except for 21 which was repainted all-over grey with red lettering. Trolley 22 had minor accident damage and was stored in Berg Isel to await repairs.

Suspension

Further air raids in 1945 caused severe damage to the overhead, and shortages in the supply of copper wire and overhead fittings enforced the suspension of the entire system. Trolleybuses were able to resume running on the section of route A between Hauptbahnhof and Hötting on 17 September 1945, and as the year drew to a close services were extended across the rest of the system. As a precautionary measure, maximum service speeds were limited to 8 km/h in areas with bomb-cratered roads, or when passing under frogs, until suitable repairs could be undertaken.

Stored trolley 22 was repaired and entered service in early 1946, painted in a dark grey and silver livery with several windows boarded over as glass was in short supply. Trolley 12 was withdrawn at the end of the 'forties and scrapped in 1955, but trolley 13 received a complete overhaul and repaint in the dark grey and silver livery. By May 1947, all three trolleybus routes were operating on 30-minute headways, reducing to 15-minutes during rush-hours.

New trolleybuses

As the wartime restrictions were gradually relaxed, six trolleybuses were ordered from Gräf & Stift in December 1947, with electrical equipment supplied by BBC. Allocated fleet numbers 23-28 they were built to a design favoured by several other Austrian systems during the late 'forties. The IVB, fearing that they would be diverted by the Russian occupation force (Russia occupied Eastern Austria from 1945-55) to their homeland if transported by rail, arranged for them to be towed all the way from Wien to Innsbruck. Trolleys 23-24 entered service on route A on 15 February 1949, but it was another fourteen months before the last of the batch arrived. Powered by a single 85-kW motor, and painted in the IVB red and white livery, they could carry 24 seated and 39 standing passengers at speeds of up to 60 km/h, and couplings were fitted for trailer operation.

One of the interesting vehicles obtained from Roma, number 12 (top) stands at the Wiltenberg terminus of route C in April 1944, the first month of trolleybus operation. The central driving position is clearly visible (W.Kreutz). An ex-Livorno trolleybus (above) passes the partly demolished Hauptbahnhof on a route B service to Pradl, 26-08-51 (J.Gillham). The former San Remo trolleys were quite modern in comparison to the others, as exemplified in this picture of number 20 at Arzl in March 1953 before taking up a duty on route B (W.Kreutz). The Livorno and San Remo vehicles were equipped with right-hand driving positions.

As business activity in the city increased, the pressure for better transport links to the commercial centre around Bozner Platz intensified. As construction costs prohibited a tramway extension, trolleybus route A was diverted via a loop running from Bozner Platz, Hochhaus and Salurner Strasse to Hauptbahnhof, and via Brixner Strasse back to Bozner Platz, on 2 December 1949.

By this time some of the pre-war trolleybuses were in poor condition. Trolley 16 was overhauled and fitted with inward folding doors, similar to those fitted to the new trolleybuses, larger and more powerful headlights and single-pane windows. It re-entered service on 12 November 1950, the same date that work began on the construction of a new trolleybus depot at Arzl.

Passenger trailers

To cater for increasing patronage on route C during peak-hours, trailers 221/3 were modified for use with trolleybuses in November 1951. These were part of a batch of seven purchased from Lohnerwerk of Wien in the autumn of 1943 to increase passenger capacity on its dwindling motor bus fleet. The first two were numbered 20-21, but were soon renumbered 224-5, and the other five were numbered 221-3/6-7. Seating was provided for 26 passengers with room for another 19 standing. Their manually-operated doors were retained, and were activated by a second conductor seated inside the trailer. Three years later, trailer 224 was similarly modified.

The fifties was a period of consolidation, but all of the former Roma vehicles had been withdrawn and

The first trolleybuses produced by Gräf & Stift after the war were built to a standard design and supplied to several Austrian undertakings. The IVB bought six and number 24 is seen departing from Hauptbahnhof on a route A service to Hötting with signs of body repairs over the rear wheel, 08-4-58. *(G. Mayr)*

scrapped by 1956. The Livorno and San Remo Fiats, however, were overhauled and modernised, the former receiving new front ends in the process, and most of the overhead wiring was replaced with new equipment supplied by Siemens.

Expansion or abandonment?

As plans for the 1964 Winter Olympics began to take shape, the IVB and certain parties in the City Council were at loggerheads over the preferred method of transporting participants between the venues in and around the city. The IVB wished to extend the trolleybus service, but this was vetoed by the Council which, quite unexpectedly, voted to abandon the trolleybus system over a period of years. The offers of second-hand trolleybuses from the undertakings of Atlanta in the USA and Münster in West Germany were not considered.

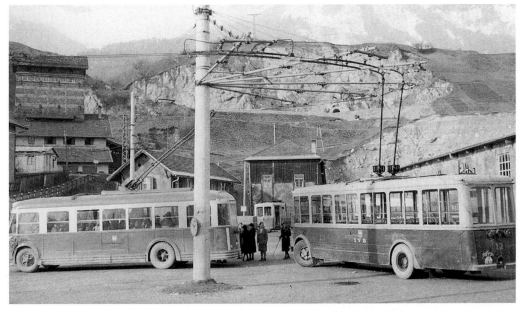

The turning loop for route C at Arzl was located directly outside the depot where passengers are preparing to board trolleybus 20 prior to its departure for Wiltenberg. Number 12 has just arrived while trolley 14, which never saw service in Innsbruck but was used as a source for spares, stands derelict in the background, 02-46. *(W.Kreutz)*

This former Livorno trolley has a reasonable load as it departs Hauptbahnhof on a route C service, 08-04-58. The rather ugly front ends on this batch of vehicles were later modernised and they continued in service until 1971. (G. Mayr)

Following an overhaul and repaint and looking distinctly smarter than in the photograph on page 59, trolleybus 24 and trailer 221 await their next duty on route A at Hötting, 08-59. (H. Wöber)

The affluent area bordering the tree-lined Kaiserjägerstrasse was served by route C until 1971 and the overhead remained in use for depot running route A trolleybuses for another five years. One of the San Remo trolleys, number 21, heads south towards the city in this September 1954 view. Today, articulated trolley -buses on route R use the same street to reach the centre. (W.Kreutz)

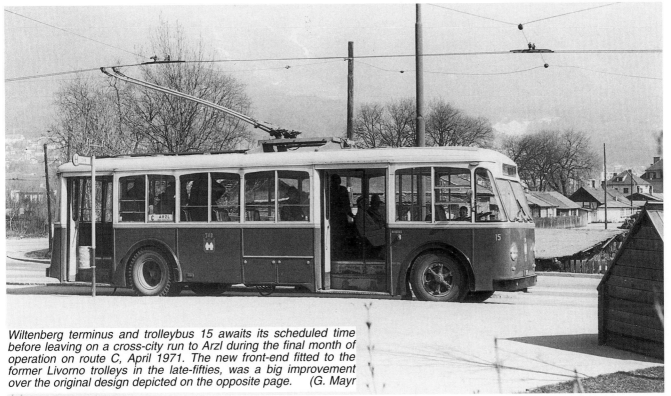

Wiltenberg terminus and trolleybus 15 awaits its scheduled time before leaving on a cross-city run to Arzl during the final month of operation on route C, April 1971. The new front-end fitted to the former Livorno trolleys in the late-fifties, was a big improvement over the original design depicted on the opposite page.   (G. Mayr

Gräf & Stift trolleybus 25 stands outside Arzl depot in the 1960s, not long after a full refurbishment and the fitting of a new-style front-end. It ran in service in this guise until the system closed in February 1976, when it was sold as a building contractor's rest room.
(collection Mackinger)

Even so, the Gräf & Stift trolleys were extensively rebuilt with new-style front-ends during 1963/4, but it was only a matter of time before the ageing fleet would have to be replaced. The Fiats were limited to 30 km/h, and service headways on route B were extended to 30-minutes on 26 May 1968, and operated by motor buses on Sundays and holidays from 1 December. Trolleybus operation on route B ceased altogether on 30 June 1969 when motor buses took over, the withdrawn trolleys being dumped behind Arzl depot.

Route C was the next to succumb to the motor bus, and this occurred on 26 April 1971. The closure of this route at this time seemed rather strange, as the overhead wiring had to remain intact between the city centre and Arzl depot to provide access for trolleybuses operating on route A. All the Fiats were now withdrawn, leaving just the six Gräf & Stift vehicles for operation on route A.

Withdrawn vehicles were disposed of as follows; Fiat 15 was stored in Arzl depot and scrapped in 1976; 16 was sold to a building contractor in 1972 and later burnt; 17-18 were sold for scrap; 19 went to the Deutschen Strassenbahnmuseum (DSM) in Hannover where it still resides; 20 became a dog kennel at a large animal park at Mentlberg; 21 joined the Eurotram museum at Klagenfurt where it is currently stored; 22 was bought by a building contractor at Zirl for use as a rest room.

Because of the excellent condition of the Gräf & Stift vehicles, route A gained a short reprieve, but only until 29 February 1976 when it was closed without ceremony. Trolleybuses 23/5/8 were sold to a building contractor in Kufstein for use as rest rooms; the electrical equipment was removed from 24 for display at Eurotram and its body scrapped; 26 joined the DSM collection; 27 went to Eurotram. At least one trailer remains available in Wilten depot, for use as a mobile rest room for IVB works staff, painted in an all-over grey livery.

To bring the section on the first trolleybus system to a close a couple of scenes showing the rebuilt Gräf & Stift trolleybuses in service. Route A operated an anti-clockwise loop through the steep, narrow and winding roads of Hötting, a suburb rising high on the north side of the river Inn. Trolley 24 (above) was a common sight on this route for many years, although they were seen on other services, such as when trolley 26 was caught on camera leaving Wiltenberg on a route C duty in April 1971.   (G. Mayr)

The trolleybus returns (1988)

Barely a decade had passed since the last trolleybus entered Arzl depot, when the Council began to debate their reintroduction. One of the major reasons for this about turn was the increasing destruction of the forests, due to rising levels of pollution from combustion-engined vehicles, and the financial inducements being offered by national government to conurbations to replace their diesel-engined buses with trams or trolleybuses.

This provided the impetus for the IVB to propose the construction of a new tram route to Olympisches Dorf, but this was blocked by the anti-tram lobby in the Council on the grounds of cost. After several acrimonious debates, the IVB announced on 28 February 1986 that trolleybuses would be used to replace buses on routes O (Olympisches Dorf) and R (Reichenau). In the November

of that year an order was placed with Gräf & Stift of Wien for 16 articulated trolleybuses, with electrical equipment from ASEA/BBC. With a length of 18 metres and powered by a single 160-kW motor, 49 seated and 93 standing passengers could be carried. A small diesel engine would provide power for use in emergencies.

The erection of overhead wiring began in March 1987 on a one-way loop running from Hauptbahnhof, and via Salurner Strasse, Maria-Theresien-Strasse to Museumstrasse, and eastwards to Pradler Strasse and Pauluskirche. At Radetzkystrasse, route R would turn right and head south to a terminus in Reichenau (Gumppstrasse), while route O would continue on, running via Reichenauer Strasse and the Grenobler Brücke to Olympisches Dorf (Josef-Kerschbaumer-Strasse). Route O would be 5.2 km long and route R 3.8 km.

A new dawn and a new Gräf & Stift trolleybus for Innsbruck. An unidentified vehicle is about to pass under the main railway line in Bienerstrasse (above) during test running in September 1988 (W.Kreutz). As there was no wiring into the depot, automatic trolley retrievers were fitted and the rear wheels turn in proportion to the amount of steering applied by the driver as an aid to getting round tight corners. The inaugural runs were made on 17 December by trolleybuses 802 and 804 and the latter awaits departure from the Olymisches Dorf route O terminus (below). *(collection Mackinger)*

Having completed the ceremonials, trolley 804 takes the left hand pair of wires for the short run back to Wilten depot from Südtiroler Platz, 17-12-88. On the right of the picture, the frontal styling of single-ended car 52 makes an interesting comparison with that on double-ended car 82.
(collection Mackinger)

Route O would follow the same route back to the railway viaduct in Museumstrasse and via Brunecker Strasse to Hauptbahnhof. Route R would return to the junction just short of Pradler Strasse where it would turn north to follow a roundabout route via Bienerstrasse, Kaiserjägerstrasse, Sillgasse and Meinhardstrasse to Hauptbahnhof. Wiring was also installed from Wilten depot along Südbahnstrasse to Hauptbahnhof to provide a link to the depot.

By the summer of 1988, sufficient trolleybuses were available to begin driver training. A press day was held on 7 September which included a ride round the central area loop, and a demonstration of emergency operation under power from the diesel engine. With fleet numbers 801-16, and painted in the standard red and cream livery, the complete batch was available by the end of the year. The cost of the completed installation was ATS 130 million.

Into service

And so, on 17 December 1988, trolleybuses 802 and 804 heralded the return of electrically-powered buses to the streets of Innsbruck less than 13 years after the demise of their predecessors with inaugural runs on routes O and R. Their large capacity and smooth ride was soon appreciated by the travelling public.

The first mishap occurred on 11 September 1989, when 816 was accidentally driven over the Schlachthof-Schleppbahn railway crossing under power from the diesel engine, but with its poles still on the wires! The 15-kV discharge from the railway overhead burst the trolleybuses's tyres and caused extensive damage to its electrical equipment, most of which was to be replaced by the manufacturer.

The system expands

The publication of the *Verkehrswissenschaftliche Konzept* (VKZ) traffic management report (see chapter 7 for more information) proposed further expansion of the trolleybus system, and could not have come at a better time for its advocates. In adopting the report's recommendations the Council outlined its own plans for the conversion of more bus routes to trolleybus operation:

Route A

Bus route A would be replaced by a trolleybus route running from Sadrach and Hötting in the west through the central area, and under routes O and R wires to the Reichenauer Strasse junction where it would split in two; one branch continuing on to Rossau and the other running via Reichenau to the DEZ shopping centre at Bleiche and the proposed P & R.

Route B

Bus route B (Hauptbahnhof to Rehgasse) would be replaced by a westerly extension of trolleybus route R.

Routes L and P

Bus routes L and P to Allerheiligen and Peerhofsiedlung, respectively, would be replaced by westerly extensions of trolleybus route O.

Ten more articulated trolleybuses, numbered 817-26, were ordered from Gräf & Stift in 1990 for operation on the new routes. Fitted with the latest electrical control equipment from Kiepe-Elektrik, and low-floor front entrances, the first vehicles arrived in May 1992 in a new livery of all-over white with red, black and grey bands round the skirt.

For the planned extensions to the west of the city, a second batch of trolleybuses was purchased from Gräf & Stift in 1992, painted in a new white livery with grey skirt. Between 1992 and 1995, route O ran via Hauptbahnhof, Triumphpforte and Anichstrasse where trolley 823 (above) silently coasts behind the unwary cyclist to the stop. (below) Route R was extended to Rehgasse in 1995 and trolleybus 809 turns from Furstenweg onto the Universitätsbrücke with an incorrect destination displayed in September 1997. *(author)*

Work on the first of the planned extensions began early in 1992 and was completed by August. Following a period of driver familiarisation, buses on routes L and P were replaced by an extension of trolleybus route O on 30 November 1992, running via Maria-Theresien-Strasse, Anichstrasse, Universitätsbrücke, Höttinger Au and Kranebitter to a junction in Lohbachsiedlung. Here the route divided into two branches; alternate duties serving Allerheiligen and Peerhofsiedlung. At 10.5 km, route O was now twice its original length.

When general traffic was re-routed away from Museumstrasse into Salurner Strasse and Maximilianstrasse in 1993, trolleybus routes O and R were diverted under new wires via Sterzingerstrasse, Heiliggeiststrasse and Leopoldstrasse on 23 August, to relieve congestion.

Work on the next bus to trolleybus conversion began early in 1995 when the poles and overhead wires were erected along Marktgraben and Innrain, and along Fischnalerstrasse and Mitterweg to Rehgasse in Höttinger Au. On 1 December 1995, twenty-six years after its conversion from trolleybus operation, bus route B was replaced by an extension of trolleybus route R, more than doubling its length to 8.4 km.

At this stage and with increasing financial constraints, the IVB was forced to bring its bus-to-trolleybus conversion programme to a premature halt, leaving the conversion of bus route A in the balance. Current proposals are for the route to be upgraded and expanded using high-capacity, low-floor buses, but this could change. Hopefully, the successful return of trolleybuses to the streets of Innsbruck and the undoubted improvements they have brought to public transport services, will encourage the IVB to reconsider this decision.

In the spring of 2000 work commenced on the erection of a second pair of overhead wires in Sillgasse, Kaiserjägerstrasse, Bienerstrasse and Pembauer-straase to enable bi-directional working of route R through this section.

Captured further down Anichstrasse as it brakes for the Bürgerstrasse stop, trolleybus 818 is operating an alternative duty on the route O branch to Peerhofsiedlung, 09-95.   (author)

The modern suburb of Hötting West is served by all services on route O and provides a high percentage of the passengers travelling to and from the city. Trolleybus 809 has just arrived from Peerhofsiedlung and about to depart on a duty to Olympisches Dorf, 08-93.   (author)

10. The routes

Tram routes

Since the closure of route 4 to Hall in 1974, the Innsbruck tramway system has remained constant, comprising urban routes 1 and 3 and interurban routes 6 and Stb. Most places of interest within, and close to the city can be reached using these routes.

Route 1: Bergisel – Hungerburgbahn — 4.9 km

Route 1 runs on a north/south axis and passes close to many well known and interesting attractions in the city.

Its southern terminus is located on the site of the former tram depot at Bergisel and comprises a single-track turning loop, layover tracks for cars on route 6, a passenger shelter and crew accommodation. The area is attractively laid out with lawns and flower beds, and nothing remains of the original depot structures.

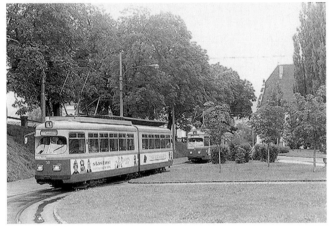

Bergisel terminus with car 38 departing on a service to Hungerburgbahn, 08-93. (author)

On leaving the terminus our car enters Klostergasse for a short run to the traffic light-controlled approach to Brennerstrasse and on crossing the junction, enters Pastorstrasse. Here the twin spires of the imposing Wilten Basilica rise high to the right, and the broad expanse of Wilten Betriebshof spreads out on our left as we brake on reaching the tram stop. The TMB museum and former Stubaitalbahnhof can be seen on the left side of the depot concourse. Accelerating away we turn sharply right and gently rise to cross the Arlberg railway on the Konzertbrücke, opened in 1956 as a replacement for the tram viaduct, and run down to the junction with Egger-Lienz-Strasse.

The trambaan in Egger-Lienz-Strasse has tram-priority traffic light control at each end. Bergisel-bound car 42, 09-95. (author)

Despite the presence of the Inntal Autobahn, this dual-carriageway is still a busy arterial ring road for much of the day, and tram drivers take extra care when crossing the eastbound lane to access the central reservation. This was the only section of segregated track on the urban routes for nearly forty years prior to 1993. We are now heading in a westerly direction and quickly build up speed. The Westbahnhof passes by on our left as we glide by the queue of traffic waiting for our car to turn right into Andreas-Hofer-Strasse under traffic light priority control.

A conventional street tramway now carries us between tall late nineteenth century dwellings and corner shops, pausing briefly at each of the four traditional pavement stops encountered on the way to the next major junction at Maximilianstrasse. Continuing on, route 1's tracks curve gently to the left and we enter Bürgerstrasse on a section of segregated track delineated by yellow lines painted on the road surface.

At the Anichstrasse junction we pass under the route R trolleybus wires and over the outbound track used by route 6 and Stb cars and note the disconnected inbound track once used by routes 1, 6 and Stb. We are now cruising along the first section of double-track tramway, installed in 1995 as part of the VKZ traffic management programme. On reaching Innrain, a sharp right turn brings us into the centrally-located tree-lined Marktplatz stop where transfers to route O trolleybuses and several bus routes can be made. Large digital panels on the two low-level platforms display destinations and departure times of the next service on each route. A confectionery kiosk and ample cover are provided for the benefit of passengers.

En-route for Bergisel, car 39 shares the Marktplatz interchange with a couple of buses, 09-98. (author)

Slowly accelerating away, our car swings right through a 100° curve into Marktgraben for 100 metres or so and then left for a similar distance before braking at the Maria-Theresien-Strasse stop. This whole area became a traffic free zone with the VKZ changes and only trams, trolleybuses, buses and taxies are allowed through it. It is one of the busiest parts of the city, with streams of tourists mingling with workers and shoppers. To the left lies the narrow Friedrich Strasse and the old quarter with its medieval arcades. To the right is the broad Maria-Theresien-Strasse with its delightful mix of department stores and little shops, and the island platform for route 3 trams.

A ring of the bell to alert pedestrians and our driver cautiously moves off into a short section of Burggraben then, as we turn right into Museumstrasse, the archway leading to the Hofburg Palace, Landestheater and Hofgarten briefly come into view to our left. A brief stop and we are heading along this straight thoroughfare, past the Landesmuseum on the left, to the junction at

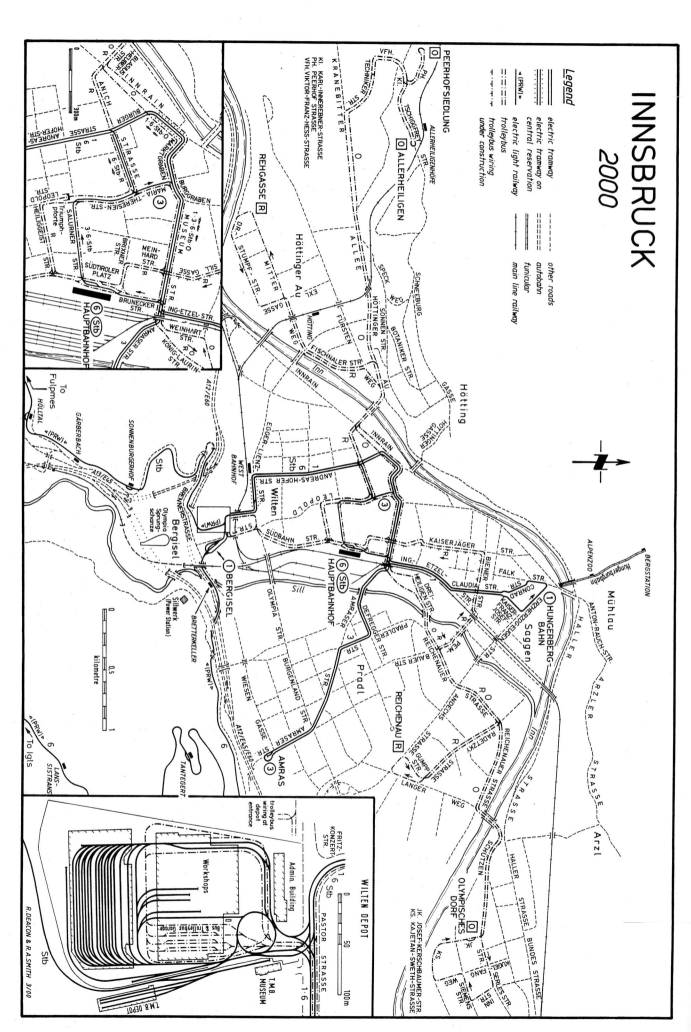

Meinhardstrasse/Sillgasse and another stop. A westbound route R trolleybus crosses in front of us as another heading east towards Reichenau turns into Museumstrasse.

As the lights go green we pull away for a short run to the next stop at the staggered crossroads formed by Brunecker Strasse on the right, up which inbound route 3, 6 and Stb cars run to Hauptbahnhof, Ing.-Etzel-Strasse to the left and, on the other side of low railway bridge ahead, Amraser Strasse with cars on route 3. The overhead wiring for trolleybus routes O and R forms part of an interesting 'spiders' web'.

Car 51 speeds alongside the railway viaduct that runs parallel to Ing.-Etzel-Strasse for much of its length, 08-93.   (author)

Under priority traffic light control, our driver moves slowly over the points, the tracks curving slightly to the right and then sharply left using a second set of points into Ing.-Etzel-Strasse, to begin a run alongside the railway viaduct with underneath, a variety of shops squeezed into snug little archways. At the Messegelände (exhibition hall), the tracks fork left into Claudia Strasse and the beginning of the affluent suburb of Saggen. The impressive looking ÖBB Bundesbahn Direktion building stands proudly on the right as the brakes are applied for

Speeding across the Bienerstrasse junction in fashionable Claudia Strasse, is car 42 heading for Bergisel, 08-93. (author)

the Bienerstrasse junction stop. A westbound route R trolleybus crosses in front of us on its way to Höttinger Au. The final section of the route takes us through an area of splendid late nineteenth century housing to a roundabout at Claudia Platz, the original terminus in 1905. Here the in- and outbound tracks diverge to form a large single-track loop along Kaiser-Franz-Joseph-Strasse and Erzherzog-Eugen-Strasse to the Hungerburgbahn terminal stop in Falkstrasse.

The lower station of the Hungerburg funicular railway is located on the north side of the junction in Rennweg, and next to it is a circular building that contains the

The Hungerburgbahn terminus of route 1 with car 37 accelerating away from the stop. The funicular station can be seen in the background, left of centre, 08-93.   (author)

Panorama der Schlacht am Bergisel, a huge painting depicting the battles fought on this southern hillside in the early nineteenth century.

Route 1 services require seven Bielefeld 6- and 8-axle cars 31/3-42/51; supplemented occasionally by Lohner cars 71-7. The first car enters service at 05:24 and is followed by cars operating a 10-minute headway between 05:34 and 06:32. This is reduced to a 7½ minute headway between 06:55 and 19:49, then increased to 20-minutes until the last car runs-in at 23:42.

An extension from Bergisel to the Olympic Pool Park&Ride is planned for construction in the near future.

Route 3: Hauptbahnhof – Amras — 4.0 km

Tram route 3 follows a figure-nine course formed by a large one-way loop through the city centre, and two-way working through the nineteenth-century suburb of Pradl to the more modern environs at Amras on the south-east extremities of Innsbruck.

The city terminus of route 3, located directly opposite the Hauptbahnhof main entrance, consists of an island platform with passenger shelter that is shared with cars on route 6. The track is single at this point prohibiting layover times of more than a few minutes. A number of stops are located on either side of the square for route R trolleybuses and various motor bus routes.

The single track Hauptbahnhof terminus of route 3 with Lohner car 76 fresh from overhaul, 09-97.   (author)

After a short wait a route 3 car arrives and disgorges its alighting passengers. Climbing up through the rear entrance, we take our seats and as the doors clunk shut, our driver moves his controller to accelerate the car slowly forward, taking the right-hand track that loops round the Stubaitalbahn terminal track, before bringing it to a halt at the light controlled junction. When the tram-only light gives the all-clear, we quickly move off, turning right into Salurner Strasse and on to the single track shared by outbound route 6 and Stb cars. Accelerating away past shops and offices, the Casino flashes by to our left as the brakes are applied for the stop by the *Triumphpforte*. This magnificent archway, which can be seen ahead of us, was erected for Maria-Theresa as a monument to her late husband in 1767 and route 3 cars passed through it until the Wiltener Platz branch closed in December 1964.

Directly ahead lies Maximilianstrasse, but we turn right into Maria-Theresien-Strasse, one of the busiest streets in the city. Bustling with shoppers and tourists, this pleasant thoroughfare boasts a fascinating variety of shops, stores, cafes and restaurants and broadens out appreciably as we approach the junction with Anichstrasse. The tracks for outbound route 6 and Stb cars branch away to our left, but we continue on into a recently semi-pedestrianised section of the street, passing by the *Annasaüle* column which was built in 1703 in honour of the victory over the Bavarians. Swinging over to the centre of the road our car comes to a stop at the island platform serving the location. Drivers often snatch a short layover here.

Three months before bi-directional operation was re-introduced in Museumstrasse and car 73 on a quiet Sunday afternoon, 09-95. (author)

The narrow confines of medieval Friedrich Strasse, and the *Goldenes Dachl* balcony, can be seen directly ahead with the beautiful Nordkette mountain range rising high in the background. We turn right into Burggraben to join the tracks of routes 1, 6 and Stb which we share as far as the east end of Museumstrasse. Having crossed the Brunecker Strasse junction, our pantograph is compressed onto the car's roof as we squeeze under the low railway bridge then turn sharply right into an island stop called Sill Park; opened in 1999 to serve the shopping complex on the far side of the street. Trolleybus routes O and R turn left at this point, and head for their destinations in the east of the city. We are now in Amraser Strasse which is quite wide for most of its length and adorned with shops on either side at this, its most northerly point. The road passes through late nineteenth century apartment blocks in Pradl all the way to the suburb of Amras.

On departing the Sill Park stop, our driver accelerates smartly away up a shallow gradient and over the river Sill into the delightful Leipziger Platz. We then leave Amraser Strasse to take a short detour through Pradl, entering Defreggestrasse on classic street tramway,

Bielefeld car 33 swings round the corner from Defreggerstrasse into Pradler Strasse, 08-93. (author)

between rows of tenement buildings, rather reminiscent of 'fifties Glasgow. On approaching the junction with Pradler Strasse, we swing over to the left, then sharply right and then left again to pull up at the Gumppstrasse stop. Moving away we continue between more tenement blocks and the Roseggerstrasse stop before re-entering Amraser Strasse. Detached, low-height properties now appear as we continue on towards Dr.-Glatz-Strasse, the one time terminus of route 3 and junction for the short-lived wartime connection into the Conradkaserne (military barracks) on the right.

The route from here to the end of the line, is on-street tramway running predominantly through modern post-war suburban housing. At Südring we cross the busy southern ring road and pass by Pradler Friedhof to the tranquil terminus at Amras. Opened in 1965, it comprises an island platform and shelter and trams reverse their direction of travel by using a tight-radius loop. To the south lie the Inntal autobahn and the lower slopes of the Patschberg forest. The return journey follows the same route as far as Museumstrasse, then via Brunecker Strasse to Hauptbahnhof.

Amras terminus with car 77 departing and 74 exiting the terminal loop. In the background, the lower slopes of Patschberg forest, 09-95. (author)

Although no plans have been published concerning the future of this route, press reports have appeared with reference to an extension to the centre of Amras village, 1 km further east. Lohner cars 71-7 are assigned to services on route 3, with occasional duties operated by Bielefeld 6-axle cars 31/3-42. The first car enters service at 05:23 and is followed by cars operating a 10-minute headway between 05:33 and 06:05, a 7¹/₂-minute headway until 20:10 and 20-minutes until the last car runs-in at 23:50.

Route 6: Hauptbahnhof – Igls — 11.8 km

Although route 6 is operated by cars of the same type as used on urban routes 1 and 3, it is a true *lokalbahn* (interurban light railway) linking the centre of the city with the village of Igls, some 300 metres higher on the Mittelgebirge plateau.

8-axle advertising car 51 on the central area loop at the Maria-Theresien-Strasse stop in Marktgraben, 09-98. *(author)*

Departing on the hour from Hauptbahnhof, our route 6 car uses the tracks in Salurner Strasse and Maria-Theresien-Strasse as far as the junction with Anichstrasse, where it turns left. A popular location for shoppers, this important street saw two-way operation of three tram routes until the Innrain extension was opened in 1995. Since then it has seen use by outbound cars on routes 6 and Stb only, the unused inbound track being disconnected at both ends. On reaching the junction with Bürgerstrasse, we turn left and join the tracks of route 1 and head for Bergisel via Andreas-Hofer-Strasse, Egger-Lienz-Strasse and Pastorstrasse.

On entering the Bergisel terminus, our driver stops the tram and alights with his point-iron to switch the points for the layover tracks that bisect the route 1 terminal loop. This location was the regular terminus for route 6 for most of its existence until 1987, when it was extended through to Hungerburgbahn. From Bergisel, the route is single track over private-right-of-way, the first section running along the side of Klostergasse, under the Brenner railway and then over the river Sill to a halt at Bretterkeller. A second track will be required to this point when route 1 is extended to the Olympic Pool Park & Ride.

A beautiful sunny day catches children eager to board car 41 as it arrives at Bergisel for a trip through the Patschberg forest to Igls, 09-95. *(author)*

Mid-winter at Tummelplatz and car 40 cruises passed the halt which is used by visitors to the nearby Schloss Ambras in the summer. *(E.Lassbacher)*

We now begin to climb up an embankment, flanked by back gardens to the left and the Inntal autobahn on the right, before turning gently right and crossing the autobahn on a tram-only viaduct; built to form part of the line's realignment back in the 'seventies. Weaving between the supporting pylons of the Brenner autobahn, we regain the old alignment and skirt the lower edge of the Patschberg Forest, all the time climbing up the south side of the Inn valley to the Tummelplatz halt, where visitors alight for the nearby Schloss Ambras. After a few minutes an abrupt right-turn takes us through a short tunnel to Schönruh, notable only for the footpaths disappearing through the trees. Accelerating gently away, we pass a huge cemetery that is almost hidden by trees as our car continues its upward journey.

Penetrating deeper into the forest and still climbing, our car negotiates a series of hairpin bends leading to the Tantegert (Auntie Gert) compulsory stop and the only passing loop on the line. Set in a clearing among the pines, the old station master's house is now in private ownership and elderly gentlemen can often be seen playing Boule behind the pretty back garden. Marked footpaths lead-off in all directions. A short layover is built into the timetable here to await the inbound tram which, after a few minutes, is heard squealing its way down through the trees and onto the track alongside ours.

Tantegert station and a vintage tram-set with goods wagon 32 loaded with mountain bikes passing blue painted car 53, 09-97. *(author)*

Pulling slowly away, we recommence our climb, the track curling through more tight hairpins and a long straight section to the Aldrans halt, which is located 1 km from the village. One final section through the trees and we burst out into open country, running along the side of a pretty grass-covered gully with views to the top of the Patscherkofel mountain to our left. Continuing on past a tiny wooden structure that is Mühlsee halt and a lake of the same name, we reach the summit of our journey at Lans-Sistrans; another popular alighting point for walkers.

The top section of route 6 runs across a flat plateau, through fields of maze and potatoes. Car 40 approaching Lanser See, 09-93. (author)

The character of the line now changes and as our car crosses open meadows on the level, stunning views across the Brenner Pass to the distant Stubai valley suddenly appear. The penultimate halt at Lanser See takes its name from a nearby lake that is a popular destination for swimmers and sunbathers in the summer. Once more, our driver pushes his controller forward and we move-off to run roadside towards Igls then forking-away to the right we enter the terminus, running round the tight-radius loop before stopping outside the station buildings. Dating from 1900, these comprise waiting room with WC and a cafe with a large terrace offering a thirst quenching coffee or beer, most welcome on a hot summer's day. For those interested in local history, the walls of the cafe are covered with photographs dating from the opening of the line.

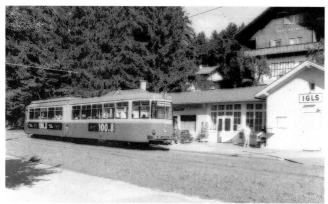

Igls terminus with car 39. The station cafe is a popular watering hole for those waiting for a tram on hot summer day, 09-98. (author)

The centre of the village is a short walk further on, but this is of no concern to our driver who takes a scheduled break before departing on his return trip to Innsbruck. Bielefeld cars 52/3 are usually assigned to services on route 6, with car 51 in reserve. For the summer schedule, the first car to Igls departs Bergisel at 06:30 and is followed by another at 07:30. A 60-minute headway is then operated from 08:00, with cars departing from Hauptbahnhof on the hour until 19:00.

The first car leaves Igls for Bergisel at 07:00 and subsequent departures operate a 60-minute headway from 08:10 until 19:10. The last car departs Igls for Bergisel at 20:00.

Throughout July, August and early September the 10:00, 12:00 and 14:00 departures from Hauptbahnhof are operated by vintage tram sets comprising a Hall bogie car, two IMB trailers and a Stb goods wagon in which bicycles can be carried. All other departures are operated by 8-axle cars 52/3 which also have provision for the carriage of cycles.

In the winter, the first car for Igls departs Bergisel at 06:30 and a 60-minute headway operates from 08:13 until the last car at 17:13. The first car leaves Igls for Bergisel at 07:00 and an hourly schedule operates from 08:45 until the last car departs Igls at 17:45.

Route Stb: Hauptbahnhof – Fulpmes — 21.0 km

The jewel in the IVB/AGStb crown (author's opinion) must be the Stubaitalbahn and a ride along its 21 km route should be included in every visitor's itinerary! Winding its way up from the Inn valley through larch and pine forests and open pastures, to the accompaniment of distant cowbells, one breathtaking view follows another in an ever-changing panorama. The friendly drivers seem to know everyone boarding their trams and they are always keen to exchange pleasantries, often via the external speakers, all of which adds to the enjoyment of the most exhilarating of tram rides.

Cars on route Stb depart from a dedicated stop outside Hauptbahnhof and share the same tracks as route 6 as far as Pastorstrasse. On arrival at Wilten Betriebshof the points automatically change to divert our

Hagen car 87 swings from Maria-Theresien-Strasse into Anichstrasse on the first leg of its run to Fulpmes, 09-95. (author)

car into the depot forecourt where a tram stop is provided by the entrance. To our left is the original depot building and the Stubaitalbahnhof, which houses the bookshop and exhibits painstakingly collated and restored by the TMB museum society. To our right is the IVB administration building and Control Centre for all IVB and AGStb services. Ahead is a double-storey trolleybus and bus depot and Central Workshop complex, the lower storey of which is out-of-site underground. The interesting track layout is based on a complete loop with tracks branching-off in every direction, while overhead, an intricate web of tram and trolleybus wiring hangs from a massive centrally-located mast, complete with clock.

We slowly move off to the accompanying sound of resetting spring-loaded points echoing across the forecourt, and climb a short ramp to the original Stb alignment between the old Stb and new IVB tram depots. The double-track grooved tramrails have now given way to single vignoles-type track on private right-of-way, and our tram begins a long steady climb, passing over the Inntal autobahn and under the Brenner autobahn in quick succession. A short run along a ridge above the former ends with a sharp left turn into a tunnel under Brennerstrasse. Still climbing, we run beside the

Car 86 turns from Pastorstrasse into Wilten depot to begin the transition from street running to private-right-of-way, 08-93.
(author)

old high road, with views across Innsbruck to the mountains beyond, to Sonnenburgerhof, where we cross the road under traffic light control and pull up at the first halt on the line. On the other side of the road to our left is a Tourist Information office and the top of the Olympic Ski jump can just be seen on the hill behind it. A passing loop was added here in 1998 in readiness for the introduction of a more frequent service.

In an instant the view has changed as we run along the side of a deep narrow gorge, signalling the beginning of the Brenner Pass. We continue climbing steadily away from the old high road and Brenner autobahn, which has appeared from twin tunnels directly below the ski jump. After a few minutes, our car takes sharp right and left turns in quick succession, passing Gärberbach halt and its vintage wooden passenger shelter, to regain its trajectory and on through some firs to the Hölltal compulsory stop. This has a small passenger shelter and passing loop and is the current crossing point with inbound service cars. Verbal exchanges between the crews, usually concerning something of interest they have noticed en-route, are a common occurrence here.

There are no signals on the Stubaitalbahn, the movement of cars being monitored by sensors buried between the rails at passing loops which transmit the information to a computer in the Control Centre. This allows the Controller to clear each driver to proceed onto the next single section of track over a radio link, the authorisation being presented on a digital display in the driver's cab. A loud beep is sounded in the cab as a car passes over a sensor on entry to a loop, and a double-beep on exiting to confirm to drivers that the sensors are working properly.

Accelerating away, our driver gives a blast on his horn and we cross the road leading up from Innsbruck, passing between modern chalet-style houses, many owned by a growing number of people using the line to commute to work, then up through a shallow valley to a compulsory stop at the village of Natters (783 m). This sleepy hamlet has expanded considerably during the last two decades. Continuing on, we turn sharply left and climb a steep escarpment leading to a small area of flat farmland and a halt at Burgstall. Opened in 1984 to serve an adjacent supermarket and nearby houses, it is located on the eastern fringe of the village of Mutters. Moving off we run along an embankment beside Innsbrucker Strasse for a short distance then take a sweeping left curve between chalets, followed by a sharp right curve, before straightening out and braking for the Mutters compulsory stop (830 m). Serving the centre of the village and equipped with a passing loop, it was one of five stops built originally with station masters' houses, waiting room and toilets. In the 1980s, the houses were sold to private owners who keep them in pristine condition. Mutters is a delightful, picturesque village and an ideal stopping-off point for exploration of the area.

The delightful little station at Mutters with car 83 departing on a Fulpmes-bound service, 09-95. *(author)*

When departing from Mutters, drivers cautiously exit the loop and give a blast on their horns to warn motorists in Innsbrucker Strasse that a tram is about to cross. Then notching up on the controller we accelerate away, running alongside Natterer Strasse for a short distance, and then curve away left onto a long section of straight track, with the village over to our left. The impressive Nockspitze mountain (2413 m) provides a perfect backdrop. The track here is laid along the edge of a steep escarpment affording excellent views over Natters down to the right. Swinging left, we slow at the approach to the Birchfeld halt, opened in 1982 to serve the

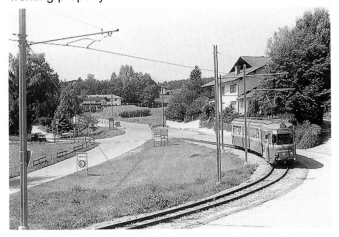

Having just left Hölltal, car 87 is about to cross Innsbruckerstrasse for the uphill run through Natters, 08-93. *(author)*

In beautiful alpine scenery, car 86 climbs above Mutters and heads for the Nockhofweg halt, 08-93. *(author)*

western fringe of Mutters and the village sports field. Another blast on the horn and we cross Götzener Strasse and climb a short ramp leading to a series of S-bends, then across the Tennis centre and Lido access road, and up a short straight to the Nockhofweg halt. Located on the southern edge of Mutters, the halt is heavily utilised in winter by skiers flocking to the nearby nursery slopes and to the Muttereralmbahn cable car for access to the steeper pistes. A steep path leads up to the Mutteralm (1608 m) and is popular with walkers during the summer months. To our left is a magnificent view over Mutters to the mountains flanking the northern side of the Inn valley.

Car 85 rumbles over the Mutterer Brücke having just emerged from the tunnel leading through from Nockhofweg in the late 'eighties. *(G. Breitfuss)*

Two roads are crossed in quick succession on leaving Nockhofweg, and the line takes on a distinct change of character. Passing first through a 250-metre-long tunnel then over a deep ravine on a curved, steel-girder bridge, it regains its upward path through beautiful open country with clusters of farms and chalets. Raitis is the first of several little hamlets along this part of the mountain and has a dedicated halt complete with modern passenger shelter. The view to our left is over the Brenner Pass towards a distant Igls and Patscherkofel mountain. Continuing on through meadow and pine forest we reach the newest halt on the line, Feldeler, opened in 1995 to serve a new housing complex. A passing loop was added a year later. On we go, to a continual *rat-tat, rat-tat, rat-tat, rat-tat* from our four bogies on the rail joints, through more meadows to a roadside halt at Ausserkreith. As we pull away we can now see beyond the imposing 260-metre-high Europabrücke (bridge), and up the Brenner towards Italy. Having crossed the road linking Kreith to Mutters, we wriggle our way round a couple of S-bends and then run up a long straight with a steep drop to our left. At

Ausserkreith and a motorist pauses at one of several unprotected crossings to allow fully-loaded car 85 to pass en-route for Innsbruck, 09-93. *(author)*

Kreith (991 m), our car takes a sharp left turn and enters the left-hand track of the passing loop. Passenger facilities here include an automatic ticket machine and a waiting room and toilets and the former station master's house. The Stubaitalbahn offers the only link between here and the Stubai valley.

Leaving Kreith behind, our car begins a shallow descent round a grassy knoll to a deep gorge, which it crosses on a steel-girder bridge, the Kreithererbrücke. Then, climbing more gently through pine and larch forests, we pass a small halt called Brandeck and on to a compulsory halt at Telfeser Wiesen (1001 m) where we await the next Innsbruck-bound tram. Set amid peaceful alpine hay meadows, the stop consists of a passing loop and bench-style seat with post-mounted timetable. Devoid of housing, this is a favourite alighting point for walkers wishing to take one of the two footpaths that parallel the line to Telfes village. After the customary exchange with the other driver, our driver accelerates away over the trailing points and onto a straight and level section of track, soon reaching the permissible 40 km/h maximum.

Through larch and pine, car 83 wends its way between Telfeser Wiesen and Luimes along the highest part of the line. *(G. Breitfuss)*

Running along the northern side of the Stubai valley, with interrupted views to the villages of Schönberg and Mieders on the far side, we wend our way through clumps of forest. Deer can be seen nervously grazing by the trees and the sound of cowbells rings-out on approaching Luimes, a tiny hamlet which at 1006 metres is the highest point on the line. The halt here has a passing loop, bench-style seat and post-mounted timetable, but no passenger shelter

Our car now passes first through a deep cutting, then under a bridge, and above a narrow road on a long sweeping left curve leading to a sharp right curve onto open pastures. The prominent spire of Telfes (994 m) church rises high above the rooftops. Telfes is a compulsory stop with passing loop and siding, and a former station master's house with adjoining waiting room, toilets and automatic ticket machine. Being a popular holiday destination, numerous pensions and guesthouses are scattered around the steep slopes of the village. From here, the line begins a steady descent across open farmland, with extensive views up the western Stubai valley. A large covered tennis complex with a dedicated halt is passed as we wind our way round a series of bends and over an unprotected crossing into Fulpmes terminus, one hour after our departure from Innsbruck.

The three-tracked terminal has changed little since it was built, comprising a former station master's house, the lower floor of which has a rest room for the tram crews, a waiting room with toilets, an automatic ticket machine and small cafe. Two tracks lead into a small depot, erected in the 1980s to house two cars overnight.

A siding is still retained at Telfes station where car 82 stops to pick passengers for the short run down to Fulpmes, 08-93.
(author)

Fulpmes (937 m) is also a popular resort and the centre, which is about 400 metres further on, has several large hotels. Passengers wishing to travel to Neustift or to villages further up the Stubai valley, can catch a bus and those seeking greater heights can take a ride up the cable car to the Kreuzjoch peak (2100 m).

Cars 82, a summer special, and 81 (in white) await their respective departure times at Fulpmes station, 09-99. (author)

Three Hagen cars (81-8) are required to operate the regular services on route Stb, predominantly on a 50-minute headway, although many additional trams are operated for enthusiasts and special parties.

On schooldays a car departs Bergisel for Kreith at 06:10 and is followed by another from Hauptbahnhof to Fulpmes at 06:44. The regular 50-minute schedule commences at 07:20 and operates until the last through service to Fulpmes at 19:40. From early July to early September, addition cars are run for the benefit of walkers heading for the mountains and shoppers heading for Innsbruck. These leave for Fulpmes at 09:38 and 16:56 and return from Fulpmes at 10:45 and 17:57 respectively. Two short-workings depart from Hauptbahnhof for Mutters at 20:30 and 21:30 followed by a third to Kreith at 22:30. This arrives back at Bergisel at 23:39.

From Fulpmes two early morning cars depart for Innsbruck at 05:40 and 06:29. The regular 50-minute schedule then commences at 07:44 and operates throughout the day until the last departure at 19:23.

Trolleybus routes

The two trolleybus services currently in operation in Innsbruck, routes O and R, were built to link the eastern suburbs with the city centre in 1988 and extended to the west in 1992 and 1995 respectively.

Route O: Olympisches Dorf - Allerheiligen/ Peerhofsiedlung — 10.5 km

The eastern terminus of route O is formed by a large clockwise-loop that wends its way through rows of apartment buildings erected on the outskirts of Innsbruck to accommodate athletes participating in the 1976 Winter Olympic Games. The terminal stop has a lay-by and passenger shelter, and is located in Josef-Kerschbaumer-Strasse at its junction with Schützenstrasse. We board our trolleybus, cancel our tickets in the machine and take a seat at the front to get the best view for our 35-minute journey.

Trolleybus 821 runs along Kajetan-Sweth-Strasse on the Olympisches Dorf loop, heading for the terminus, 08-93.
(author)

At the scheduled time, our driver closes the doors and pulls away, turning left into Schützenstrasse for a run through the *village* to Haller Strasse flyover at a point once traversed by tram route 4. We turn sharp left onto the Grenobler Brücke and cross the river Inn, then turn right into Reichenauerstrasse past the Jugendherberge (youth hostel) to the junction with Radetzkystrasse. Here trolleys on route R turn from Radetzkystrasse and share the wires with route O as far as Pembaurstrasse. Westbound route R trolleybuses turn right here but we continue on, stopping briefly to pick up passengers at the Pradler Strasse stop, then over the river Sill and into Dreiheiligenstrasse, where the inbound and outbound wires separate to follow a one-way system to Weinhartstrasse.

Emerging from the railway bridge in Museumstrasse, trolleybus 826 crosses tram route 3's tracks to enter König-Laurin-Strasse, under the watchful gaze of a couple of young budding drivers, 08-93.
(author)

Under traffic light control we pull away and turn right, our trolleybooms almost touching the roof as we pass under the low railway bridge, and into Museumstrasse. At the Sillgasse junction, route R trolleys heading west cross from the right, but we continue on via the Landesmuseum stop, turning left on reaching Burggraben and continue on to the busy Maria-Theresien-Strasse stop. On moving off we take a sharp right turn and run for a hundred metres to the junction with Innrain, and turn left under traffic light priority into the Marktplatz interchange. Several passengers alight from the centre and rear doorways while others board at the front.

Marktplatz and trolleybus 820 stops at the interchange while in the background a tram on route 1 waits to turn into Marktgraben, 09-98. *(author)*

We now follow the path of former trolleybus route C between tall late nineteenth century buildings to a stop called Klinik; used by people heading for the nearby hospital and students attending the University building across the junction. We turn right here into Blasius-Heuber-Strasse and share the wires with route R trolleys exiting Anichstrasse to cross the river Inn on the Universitätsbrücke, turning left into Höttinger Au on reaching the north bank. After a few hundred metres the westbound route R trolleybus wires branch-off left into Layrstrasse, but we continue on passing under the Karwendelbahn railway bridge to a stop called Am Giesen.

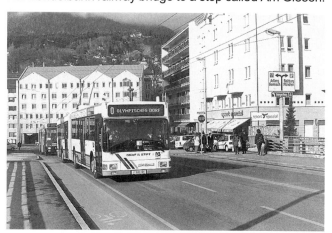

Trolleybus 820 makes the first of two crossings of the river Inn on its way from Allerheiligen to the city, Universitätsbrücke. *(collection Mackinger)*

We are now in Kranebitter Allee which for the next kilometre or so comprises two bi-directional carriageways separated by a row of mature trees. While through traffic makes use of the newer wider section, trolleybuses treat each carriageway as one-way working, westbound trolleys making do with the original narrow road. To the right is the sprawling suburb of Lohbachsiedlung, while over on the left is the airport

which we parallel all the way to the next junction at Technikerstrasse. Turning right here, we run along a dual-carriageway and into Hötting West. Another right turn brings us into the Victor-Franz-Hess-Strasse precinct and a stop close to a row of small shops.

The route is now uphill and on reaching the Peerhofstrasse junction, divides into two, alternate duties serving each branch. The Allerheiligen service continues its climb, turning into the narrow Tschig-gfreystrasse to a terminal loop at St Georgsweg, just short of a level crossing on the Karwendelbahn. This pleasant suburb has an abundance of large detached houses. Back down the road, the Peerhofsiedlung service turns left into Peerhofstrasse and winds its way up to a very tight turning loop strung from modern apartment buildings.

Located among modern apartment blocks, the Peerhofsiedlung terminal loop is extremely tight. Trolleybus 816 lays-over, 08-93. *(author)*

The other western branch of route O terminates outside a church in the hillside suburb of Allerheiligen, seen here with trolleybus 818, 08-93. *(author)*

Route O is operated by the 1992 batch of trolleybuses with some duties provided by the earlier batch. Early morning short-workings leave Olympisches Dorf for the city centre at 05:00 and 05:25 with the first through services to Peerhofsiedlung and Allerheiligen departing at 05:35 and 05:45 respectively. An early short-working leaves Allerheiligen for the city at 05:00 followed by the first through services to Olympisches Dorf from Allerheiligen at 05:38 and Peerhofsiedlung at 05:48. A 6-minute headway operates for much of the day, with alternate services using the two branches two Allerheiligen and Peerhofsiedlung, extending to 20-minutes in the evenings.

The last departure from Olympisches Dorf to Peerhofsiedlung leaves at 19:33; arriving at 20:04, while the final through service to Allerheiligen departs at 23:42;

arriving at 00:11. The last through trolleybus from Peerhofsiedlung departs at 19:46; arriving at Olympisches Dorf at 20:16, while the last Allerheiligen - Olympisches Dorf trolley leaves at 23:45; arriving at 00:16. A short-working to the city centre departs Allerheiligen at 00:20; arriving at Landesmuseum at 00:36.

Route R: Reichenau - Höttinger Au — 8.4 km

The Reichenau terminus of route R is situated in side-street called Gumppstrasse and is accessed via a triangular-shaped clockwise-loop that passes round a cluster of low-rise apartment blocks. The trolleybus service is popular with people visiting the extensive semi-covered Bleiche shopping centre nearby. Precisely on time, our driver closes the doors and accelerates

Two trolleybuses, 812 nearest, at Reichenau terminus not long after route R's conversion from diesel to electric operation. Note the single rear wheels and trolley retrievers.
(collection Mackinger)

slowly away, turning left into Radetzkystrasse, to head north between rows of early post-war urban housing stock. Two stops are encountered on the way to the junction with Reichenauerstrasse, where we turn left to join the wires of route O as far as Pembaurstrasse.

At this point, westbound route R trolleys turn right to follow a sweeping semi-circular course on a one-way loop through leafy northern suburbs, crossing first the river Sill on a humped-back bridge, then passing through a narrow arch under the main ÖBB railway line, and on by the Bundesbahn Direktion building to the junction with Claudia Strasse. When the lights go green, we move off and cross the tracks of tram route 1 into Bienerstrasse, a pleasant avenue bordered by mature trees and large residential properties. Kaiser-jägerstrasse lies directly ahead and we turn left into it and head south towards the city centre. On reaching

Having passed through the low archway under the mainline railway, the driver of trolleybus 808 prepares to stop at Bundesbahn Direktion, 08-93. *(author)*

Universitätsstrasse, we turn sharp right quickly followed by a left into Sillgasse between rather drab buildings to a stop at the junction with Museumstrasse. Here we rejoin eastbound route R trolleybuses one of which can be seen turning into Museumstrasse ahead. It will share the wires with route O trolleys via a more direct route back to Radetzkystrasse.

When the lights go green we cross the tram tracks into Meinhardstrasse, close to the commercial heart of the city and turn left into Brixner Strasse at the next junction. This takes us into Süd Tiroler Platz and a busy stop located on the opposite side of the square to Hauptbahnhof. As we move away, a departing route 3 tram pulls alongside an Stb car laying-over on the central reservation, and we cross Salurner Strasse into Sterzinger Strasse, passed the large Postbus bus station on the left-hand side. Turning right into the relative quiet of Heiliggeiststrasse, our driver accelerates between

Trolleybus 804 has passed through the Triumphpforte archway and is heading up Leopoldstrasse on its way to Hauptbahnhof and Reichenau, 09-97. *(author)*

attractive rows of period apartment buildings and on reaching the end of the street, makes a right turn into Leopoldstrasse and Triumphpforte. We skirt round the memorial, but eastbound trolleys pass through the narrow archway, just as the trams did until 1964. We are now heading north along Maria-Theresien-Strasse sharing the street with route 6 and Stb trams, and turn left on reaching Anichstrasse. At Bürgerstrasse the trams turn left but we continue along Anichstrasse to the Klinik stop, just short of the junction with Innrain.

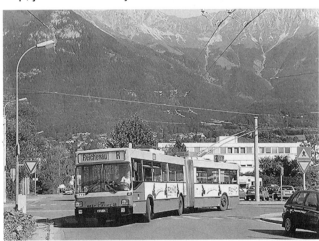

Trolleybus 804 swings from Mitterweg into Exlgasse at the beginning of a long one-way loop through the quiet suburb of Höttinger Au, 09-97. *(author)*

Across the junction and over the Universitätsbrücke we go, once again sharing the wires with trolleys on route O. At Layrstrasse we turn left and on into Fischnalerstrasse, a long road curving gently to the right. Many of the low-rise apartment buildings that spread-out on the right are home to students and the river Inn may be spotted through the trees lining the embankment to the left. At Holzhammerstrasse we cross the junction and enter Mitterweg the first part of which is dominated by light industry. Shortly after passing under a railway bridge we reach Exlgasse where we turn left followed by a right into Dr.-Stumpf-Strasse, and begin a run up one side of an elongated terminal loop to the Rehgasse terminus. The area comprises modern housing in a pleasant suburban setting on the edge of Höttinger Au, due south of the airport. After a short layover, our driver will move off and re-enter Mitterweg to start another cross-city journey to Reichenau.

Route R is operated by the 1988 batch of trolleybuses. Short-workings from the city centre to Rehgasse are operated at 05:19, 05:39 and 05:49 followed by the first through service from Reichenau at 05:35. A 10-minute schedule operates for much of the day, extending to 20-minutes in the evenings. The last through service to Rehgasse leaves Reichenau at 22:50; arriving at 23:21, followed by short-workings from the centre to Rehgasse at 23:10 and 23:30.

The Rehgasse terminus with trolleybus 812 about to take-on its first passengers for the cross-city run to Reichenau, 09-97.
(author)

In the opposite direction, short-workings depart from the city centre for Reichenau at 05:17, 05:27 and 05:37 followed by the first through service from Rehgasse at 05:33. The last through trolley to Reichenau leaves Rehgasse at 22:46; arriving at 23:11, followed by short-workings from the centre to Reichenau at 23:06 and 23:26.

Route 4: Innsbruck - Hall

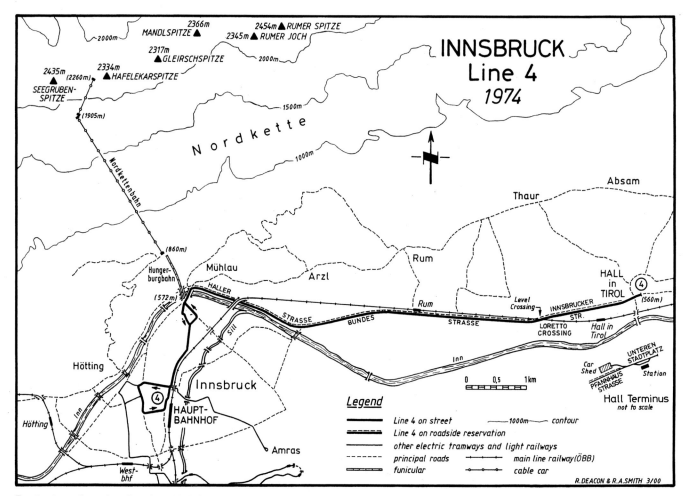

Route 4 ran from Innsbruck to Hall from 1891 until its closure in 1974.

Cable-cars and a funicular

In addition to trams and trolleybuses, Innsbruck possesses three cable-car lines and a funicular. Located within easy reach of a local tram stop, they offer stunning views of Innsbruck, the Inn valley, the Brenner Pass and mountain peaks up to 50 km away.

To the north, a route 1 tram to the Hungerburgbahn terminus provides a convenient transfer point for the funicular railway and a ride up the lower slopes of the Hungerburg for onward connection with the Nordkettenbahn cable-car line. Alternatively, a visit to the Alpine Zoo is a short walk from the middle station on the funicular.

To the south of the city, route 6 trams stop at Schloss Ambras for people visiting the nearby castle, and a ride through the forest to Igls gives access to the Patscherkofelbahn cable-car line. The battlefield memorial and famous Olympic Ski Jump are located at Bergisel, a short uphill climb from the terminus of route 1. The Ski Jump can also be reached from the Sonnenburgerhof halt on the Stubaitalbahn (Stb) tram route.

Further up on the Stb is the Nockhofweg halt, the alighting point for the lower terminus of the Muttereralmbahn cable-car line, although it is only in operation during the ski season. For panoramic views, a ride on an Stb car to Fulpmes is very rewarding.

Nostalgiefahrten

During the summer months, a special tram service operates on Wednesday afternoons for the benefit of tourists wishing to experience a ride on an historic tram-set over the Stubaitalbahn. Comprising a Hall bogie car and four veteran open-platform trailers it departs Bergisel at 13:15, for Fulpmes where it arrives just after 14:00. It then departs from Fulpmes at 14:26 for the return trip to Hauptbahnhof. At 18:03 the same tram-set leaves Hauptbahnhof for a second round-trip to Fulpmes.

Route 6 services departing from Hauptbahnhof at 10:00, 12:00 and 14:00 through the Patschberg forest to Igls are operated using vintage tram-sets from the end of June to the beginning of September. For the price of a single ticket, bicycles are carried in an elderly goods wagon and crews for these services are provided by volunteers from the TMB museum society

Facts and figures

The number of passengers travelling on the 21 trams, 26 trolleybuses and 99 buses on IVB urban services has remained constant; the total for 1999 exceeding 42 million. Over 45% of these were carried on the electrically-operated tram and trolleybus services of which the former constitutes 16.5 km of the overall route length, compared with 18.6 km for the trolleybuses and 156 km for buses. In the same year, the 8 trams operating on the 21-km Stubaitalbahn line carried over 900 000 passengers.

"SMARTINFO"

Using the slogon "Informed passengers are contented passengers", the IVB introduced its first digital passenger information displays with the opening of the Marktplatz interchange in 1995, and similar displays are progessively being installed at other major stops and interchange points around the system. Originally known as PACOS (Passenger Information and Coordination System), and more recently as SMARTINFO, the Siemens-built displays show the routes serving a particular stop, the ultimate destination and anticipated time of arrival of the next vehicle on each route. Times are displayed in minutes for vehicles fitted with the IBIS identification and location system or as scheduled arrival times for vehicles without. The displays are also used to convey information on delays caused by traffic hold-ups, accidents and breakdowns.

A glorious sunny day and the 14:26 'Nostalgiefahrt' from Fulpmes has arrived at Telfes to pick up more passengers taking the vintage tram ride to Innsbruck. The same tram set will bring them back in the evening. (collection Mackinger)

Winter in the Tirol can be extremely bitter and heavy snow falls play havoc with the tramway and the mountain lines in particular. Car 86 (above) had a lucky escape near Luimes on the Stubaitalbahn when a tree fell across its path, bringing down the overhead and stranding it until a works car could be brought up from Innsbruck, 11-02-84. (E. Plefka) Despite the atrocious conditions at Tantegert (below), a route 6 Hall car is still able to operate, the tracks having been cleared sufficiently by snowbroom 200.

(W.Kreutz)

Tickets and Fares

IVB Tarife

Tickets for travel solely on IVB services can be selected from two categories; a specified number of journeys or a period of time. Tickets in the latter category give good value for money as they offer unlimited travel on any IVB service within the selected time band. For example, passengers wishing to make occasional journeys can purchase single- or 4-ride tickets, whereas those using the system for daily travel to and from work would probably buy an annual ticket. A recent addition, called PLUS-Tarife, offers a ticket that allows up to four children to accompany one adult at an all-inclusive price. As the Tarife is usually changed annually, the 1999 prices listed in the table below should only be used as a guide.

Ticket type	Duration	Price(ATS)	Limitations
Einzelticket	1-journey	21,-	purchase from driver only
Einzelticket, ermassigt	1 journey	12,-	children under 15
4-Fahrtenticket	4 journeys	60,-	
4-Fahrtenticket, ermassigt	4 journeys	47,-	children under 15
Tagesticket	Day of purchase	33,-	
24-Stundenticket	24 hours	45,-	
24-Stundenticket, ermassigt	24 hours	34,-	children under 15
24-stundenticket PLUS	24 hours	98,-	+4 children under 15
Wochenticket	7 days	115,-	
Monatsticket	1 month	415,-	
Monatsticket Senior	1 month	310,-	senior citizens
Halbjahresticket	6 months	2150,-	
Halbjahresticket Senior	6 months	1600,-	senior citizens
Jahresticket	12 months	4300,-	
Jahresticket Senior	12 months	3200,-	senior citizens

Notes:

a   Up to two children under the age of 6 can travel free when accompanied by an adult and when not occupying a seat.

b   Ermassigt tickets are at reduced rates and additionally include school children, the mobility impaired, the blind, and senior citizens living in Innsbruck.

c   Bicycles are carried on all services at a flat 21,- rate.

d   Dogs and other small animals are carried free of charge.

e   School and youth groups of up to 20 people under the age of 19 can purchase tickets at reduced (ermassigt) rates.

The *Innsbruck* Card

The most economical way of travelling around town and the mountains beyond is to purchase an Innsbruck Card. Of credit card size it is valid for 24-, 48-, or 72-hour periods and costs ATS 230, 300 or 370 (year 2000 prices), respectively, per person; children half price. Validation begins from the time of first use and it gives all-inclusive access to most museums, palaces and historic sites. A major benefit is that the cost of travel on all IVB public transport services within the town is included, as are trips on tram route 6 to Igls, the Stubaitalbahn as far as Sonnenburgerhof, the Hungerburgbahn funicular railway and the Patscherkofel and Nordkette cable-car lines. Innsbruck Cards can be purchased at the Tourist Information office at Burggraben 3 and the tourist offices in Mutters and Igls.

A one-way ride on the Stubaitalbahn from Hauptbahnhof to Fulpmes costs 50,-, but if several journeys are planned, a weekly ticket offers unlimited travel for the whole line and is excellent value at ATS 148,-. Weekly tickets can be purchased from the Mutters and Innsbruck tourist offices and the automatic ticket machines located at the main Stb stations.

Passenger figures

	1995	1996	1997	1998	1999
Route 1	6 348 540	5 987 234	5 555 571	5 437 237	5 506 825
Route 3	4 897 111	4 617 837	4 284 904	3 760 756	3 806 749
Route 6	371 481	350 105	324 863	350 125	355 053
Route Stb	968 763	947 014	905 404	874 893	903 289
Route O	11 278 108	10 631 661	9 865 149	11 603 560	11 746 062
Route R	3 415 879	5 202 823	4 827 714	5 078 874	5 141 107
Bus services	20 772 730	17 618 450	16 331 812	15 037 169	15 291 080
HBB	608 437	451 138	509 425	515 072	487 648
TOTAL	48 661 049	45 806 262	42 604 842	42 657 686	43 237 813

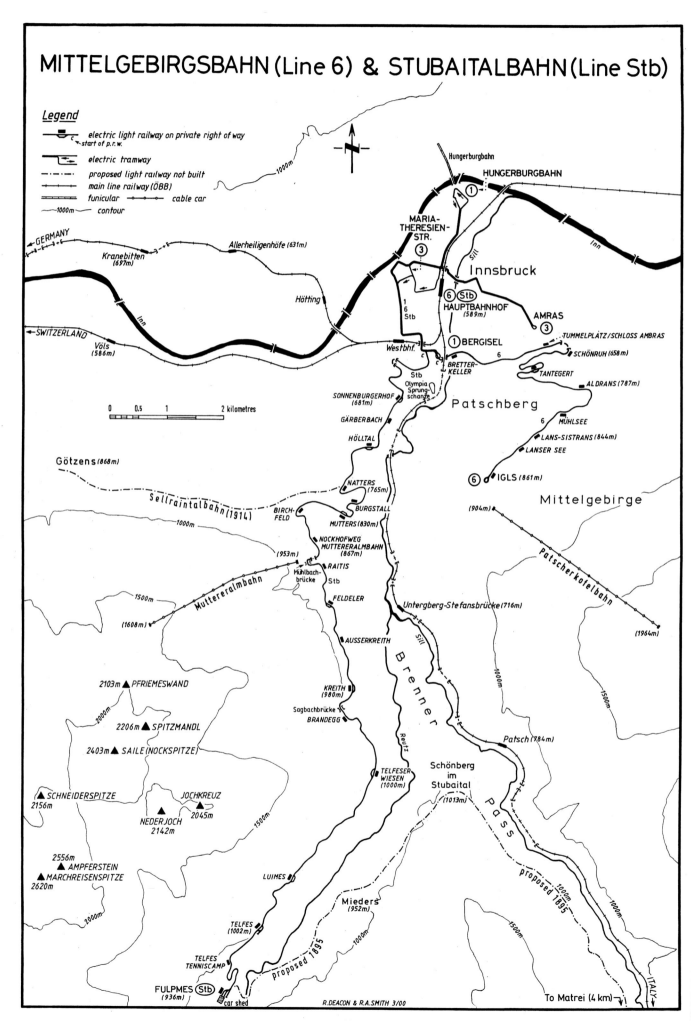

MITTELGEBIRGSBAHN (Line 6) & STUBAITALBAHN (Line Stb)

Legend

electric light railway on private right of way
start of p.r.w.
electric tramway
proposed light railway not built
main line railway (ÖBB)
funicular — cable car
1000m — contour

Hungerburgbahn

HUNGERBURGBAHN

①

MARIA-
THERESIEN-
STR.
③

Innsbruck

Inn

Sill

GERMANY

Kranebitten
(697m)

Allerheiligenhöfe (631m)

Hötting

1
6
Stb

⑥ Stb
HAUPTBAHNHOF
(589m)

AMRAS
③

SWITZERLAND

Völs
(586m)

Inn

Westbhf.

① BERGISEL

c

Stb

BRETTER-
KELLER

6

TUMMELPLÄTZ/SCHLOSS AMBRAS

SCHÖNRUH (658m)

TANTEGERT

AL DRANS (787m)

Patschberg

SONNENBURGERHOF
(681m)

Olympia
Sprung-
schanze

GÄRBERBACH

6 MÜHLSEE

LANS-SISTRANS (844m)

HÖLLTAL

LANSER SEE

Götzens (868m)

⑥ IGLS (861m)

Mittelgebirge

NATTERS
(765m)

(904m)

Sellraintalbahn (1914)

BIRCH-
FELD

BURGSTALL

MUTTERS (830m)

1000m

Patscherkofelbahn

NOCKHOFWEG
MUTTERERALMBAHN
(867m)

(953m)

Mühlbach-
brücke

RAITIS

Stb

1500m

Muttereralmbahn

FELDELER

Untergberg-Stefansbrücke (716m)

(1608m)

AUSSERKREITH

Sill

Brenner

(1964m)

2103m ▲ PFRIEMESWAND

KREITH
(980m)

Sagbachbrücke

BRANDEGG

Reutz

1000m

1500m

2206m ▲ SPITZMANDL

2403m ▲ SAILE (NOCKSPITZE)

Patsch (784m)

▲ SCHNEIDERSPITZE
2156m

JOCHKREUZ

▲
NEDERJOCH
2142m

▲
2045m

TELFESER
WIESEN
(1000m)

Schönberg
im
Stubaital

Pass

(1013m)

proposed 1895

2556m
▲ AMPFERSTEIN
▲ MARCHREISENSPITZE
2620m

LUIMES

1000m

1000m

Mieders
(952m)

2000m

1500m

proposed 1895

1000m

TELFES
(1002m)

TELFES
TENNISCAMP

FULPMES Stb
(936m)

car shed

R.DEACON & R.A.SMITH 3/00

To Matrei (4 km)

ITALY

11. Current rolling stock

Tramcars

Terminology

With the advent of articulated tramcars a classification system was introduced to identify the different types; usually in terms of the number of axles. In tramway parlance the German for 'articulated motor car' is *Gelenk Triebwagen*. The system takes the letters G and T and adds the number of axles to define the type of car. A 6-axle articulated car, for example, is classified as type GT6, although this may be revised to 6xGelER or 6xGelZR to further identify the same car as articulated and single-ended or double-ended; ER=Einrichtung, ZR=Zweirichtung, Gel=Gelenk (articulated).

Articulated trams also comprise a number of body-sections; two sections on 6-axle cars and three on 8-axle cars in Innsbruck's case. These are designated A for the front, B for the rear and C for the centre.

give them a marked resemblance to the American PCC car. Four sets of double doors are fitted to the GT8 version (three on a GT6) and passengers can enter at the second, third and fourth pairs. Seating is provided for 37 passengers and up to 78 standing passengers can be carried. The electrical equipment was supplied by Kiepe, and single Garbe-Lahmeyer 100-kW BG 75 motors were fitted to the front and rear trucks.

The first three cars to arrive in Innsbruck comprised one GT6 (ex-825) and two GT8 (ex-812 and 814), and car 812 made the first test run over route 1 on 28 August 1980 still in its Bielefeld livery. Its C (centre) section was then removed for transfer to Hagen car 87, and the A (front) and B (rear) sections reformed to produce a GT6 type car. Following a full overhaul and repaint it entered service on 25 March 1981 as car 31, the first of a new series. The second GT8 car, number 814, was overhauled and its C section removed, prior to entering service as car 32 in April 1981.

Purchased by the IVB in 1982, former Bielefeld 8-axle car 802 was converted to 6-axle configuration in Wilten depot and renumbered 41 before entering service in Innsbruck five years later. In this view, it is passing over the points leading into the depot from Pastorstrasse on a route 1 service to Bergisel, 09-97.   (author)

This chapter gives an historical and technical summary of the rolling stock currently operated by the Innsbrucker Verkehrsbetriebe.

Type GT6/8: 31/33 - 42/51 - 53

When Bielefeld began to replace its fleet of 40 GT6 and GT8 cars in 1980 the IVB seized the opportunity to continue with its modernisation programme, and purchased fifteen cars between 1980 and 1983.

Built by Düwag in 1957/62-3, these single-ended cars have doors on the nearside only and front and rear body styling considerably different from the double-ended Hagen design. Their split sloping windscreens

A further six GT8 cars, 801/2/10/1/3/5, were purchased from Bielefeld in July/August 1982 followed by two more GT8 cars, 803/5, and four GT6 cars 822-4/40 towards the end of 1983. Nine of these cars entered service in GT6 configuration during the 1980s, the C sections having first been removed from the GT8 cars for transfer to the Hagen cars. Two cars, 801/3, retained their C sections and were equipped with dead-man controls and higher-rated braking resistors for operation on route 6. Renumbered 51/2, respectively, they entered service in April 1985/October 1986 on the urban routes until the installation of a turning circle at Igls, completed in May 1987, enabled them to operate on route 6.

Bielefeld 8-axle car 803, purchased in 1983, retained its centre section on entering service in Innsbruck as car 52 in 1986. Intended primarily for operation on route 6 to Igls, it sees occasional use on urban route 1 and is captured here at the Bergisel terminus.
(collection Mackinger)

The modifications required for one-man operation involved the installation of ticket cancelling machines, driver-controlled automatic door operation, external loudspeakers, internal public address systems and improved ventilation for the driver. Modified cars were identified by the word SCHAFFNERLOS (conductor-less) in white on a broad blue band below the rear, side and front windows.

GT6 cars 31/38-42 subsequently received modifications for operation on the Igls route, but their low passenger capacity led to severe overcrowding during rush-hours. The problem was eased a little when the centre section from another Bielefeld car, 809, was purchased and fitted to GT6 car 32 as it passed through overhaul. Renumbered 53, and re-equipped for operation on the Igls route, it re-entered service in November 1991.

To cover for a possible shortage of rolling stock during the Hagen car refurbishment programme, a start was made in 1989 to prepare Bielefeld GT6 car 823 for service. It had languished in Wilten depot for several years, and much of its equipment had been removed for fitment to other cars, so accident damaged car 837 was purchased from Bielefeld to provide a source of spare parts. The rebuild took two years to complete and car 823 entered service as number 42 on 13 November 1990. The remnants of car 837 were scrapped leaving only car 824 in store, but it too was stripped of useful parts and sent to the breakers in 1993.

To attract more visitors onto the Igls line car 53 was painted in a silver, blue and white livery in the spring of 1997, and adorned with images portraying the attractions and beauty of the Mittelgebirge. It was also equipped with a cycle rail in place of the conductors desk in the rear, a facility much appreciated by local people and visitors wishing to ride the mountain pathways.

To assess the appearance of the GT6 cars in the new all-white livery, car 40 was repainted white in May 1998, and several more have been similarly treated. Car 31 was also painted white and decorated with cultural images as a tourist attraction, and GT8 car 51 became the first all-over advertising car when it was painted with the red and white logos of a prominent city store.

Basic details of the ex-Bielefeld cars are listed in the table below:

IVB No.	Type	Built	In IVB service	ex-SBV C-section	ex-SBV No.
31"	6xGelER	1962	19.03.81		812
32""*	6xGelER	1962	21.04.82		814
33"	6xGelER	1957	05.08.82		825
34"	6xGelER	1962	06.02.83		811
35"	6xGelER	1957	09.08.83		810
36"	6xGelER	1962	16.02.84		815
37"	6xGelER	1957	09.09.84		822
38"	6xGelER	1963	02.04.86		805
39"	6xGelER	1962	04.04.86		840
40"	6xGelER	1962	24.03.87		813
41"	6xGelER	1963	14.07.87		802
42"	6xGelER	1957	13.11.90		823
51'''	8xGelER	1963	17.04.85	801	801
52"	8xGelER	1963	24.10.86	803	803
53'''	8xGelER	1962	13.11.90	809	814

* Car 32 was converted to 8-axle and renumbered 53 in 1991.

Type GT6: 71 - 77

The successful introduction of bogie cars 61-6 in 1960 paved the way for the subsequent modernisation of Innsbruck's tram fleet. To replace the veteran Basel 2-axle cars, seven GT6 single-ended articulated tramcars were ordered from Lohner in Wien in 1965.

Built under licence from Düwag and numbered 71-7, the first car arrived in Innsbruck on 29 July 1966. Externally they were similar to the bogie cars and could carry 43 seated and 72 standing passengers in a 19.4 metre-long body. Painted in the red and white livery they had an abundance of chrome trim.

Powered by two Elin BG 75 100-kW motors, these splendid vehicles completed the modernisation on the urban routes, although two ex-Zürich cars continued to operate as rush-hour extras on route 1 for a further decade. Unlike their German cousins, the Lohner cars were fitted with single-width front entrances with three-quarter-length glazed doors to improve driver vision at tram stops, and narrower saloon windows than the Düwag cars. Passengers entered at the rear and purchased a ticket from a seated conductor.

62. The conversion involved removal of the conductors desks and fitting cash and ticket dispensing equipment alongside the driver. One-man cars were identified by broad blue bands below the rear, side and front windows with the word SCHAFFNERLOS in white. The rest of the cars in this batch were similarly converted as they passed through overhaul between 1990-2.

As part of a cost cutting exercise, cars 74/7 were placed in store in 1995, their working days seemingly over. Car 74, however, was given a full overhaul and returned to service in early 1998, and was followed by car 77 in the white livery later in the year. Most of the batch have had the four rear-most seats removed to allow for the fitting of cycle rails.

A fine study of car 76 heading east along Amraser Strasse on a route 3 service to Amras. These Lohner-built cars are distinguished from their Düwag-built cousins by the single front door, headlight arrangement and chrome trim. (TMB)

IVB No.	Type	Built	In IVB service
71	6xGelER	1966	08.11.66
72	6xGelER	1966	08.11.66
73	6xGelER	1966	08.11.66
74	6xGelER	1966	08.11.66
75	6xGelER	1966	1966
76	6xGelER	1966	1966
77	6xGelER	1967	1967

Route 3 was the regular haunt for these cars for many years, although they did occasionally stray on to route 1. Car 76 was the first of the batch to be converted for one-man operation, and it re-entered service on 20 December 1989 on the trucks from scrapped bogie car

Type GT8: 81 - 88

When the Hagen tramways closed in 1976 its fleet of 26, Düwag-built, GT6 tramcars were offered for sale. Dating from 1959 to 1967, and with fleet numbers 60-85, they were rugged, reliable vehicles, and maintained to a very high standard. The IVB purchased eight cars, numbered 62-9, which dated from 1960/1.

The first four cars for Innsbruck arrived by rail on 18 August 1976 and were joined by the remainder shortly after. Following inspection and preparation, they were repainted red and cream and renumbered 82-9. Car 86 was completed first and made a test run through the town on 13 October. A period of crew familiarisation then preceded the entry into service of the first Hagen cars on route 1 on 13 December.

With the arrival of the first Bielefeld 8-axle cars in 1980, the IVB began to implement its operating strategy of modifying the Hagen cars for use on the interurban routes to Igls and Fulpmes. Clearance tests using car 84 had been carried out over the lower section of route 6 in April 1977, in anticipation of the change, and further tests followed in 1979 using car 89.

The problem of the low passenger capacity of the Hagen cars, which at 113 was approximately two-thirds that of a five-car motor and trailer unit then operating on the Igls line, was resolved by transferring the centre sections from the Bielefeld cars, raising their capacity to 61 seated and 93 standing passengers. Car 87 was the first Hagen car converted to 8-axle, when it received the C section from Bielefeld car 812 in August 1980. It was equipped with dead-man controls and higher rated braking resistors and began trial running on the Igls line on 17 November. GT6 cars 85/9 received the same electrical modifications early in the following year as preparations continued for the replacement of the ageing rolling stock used on route 6, which occurred on 19 February 1981.

The second Hagen car to be converted to GT8 standard was car 83, which received the C section from Bielefeld car 814. It was fitted with modified electrical and braking systems and entered service on route 6 on 8 March 1982, releasing car 85 for use on the urban routes.

Following an abortive attempt to obtain some former Hagen cars from Beograd the IVB decided to modify more Bielefeld cars for operation on the Igls line, and transfer all Hagen cars to the Stubaitalbahn. Car 82 was taken into the workshops and equipped with modified electrical and braking systems, pneumatic sanders, and

fitted with the C section from Bielefeld car 815. Both it and cars 83 and 86, the latter fitted with the C section from car 811, took over the services on the Stb on 2 July 1983, supported by car 85 (fitted with the C section from car 810) by the end of the month.

The three remaining Hagen GT6 cars re-entered service after conversion to GT8 on the following dates; car 84 (C section from car 813) – 21 December 1983; car 89 (C section from car 805) – November 1984 (when it was renumbered 81); car 88 (C section from car 802) – 19 January 1985.

When it failed to obtain financial backing for new trams in 1988, the IVB contracted Bombardier-Rotax to refurbish the Hagen cars, and car 84 was dispatched to Wien by rail on 25 August 1989. It was used as the prototype for the rest, and remained in the capital for fifteen months. Externally, little was changed — twin headlights and a centrally mounted roof light were fitted, to conform to regulations governing light railways, and the logo "STUBAITALBAHN A.G." was applied in white across the dash. To reduce glare, tinted glass windscreens with black trim replaced the original plain glass versions, and new body panels were fitted throughout. Internally, more comfortable padded seating replaced the original plastic variant, and the conductors desks were reinstalled in such a way as to allow their easy removal when the change to one-man operation was implemented on the Stb. Car 84 re-entered service on 23 November 1990. Using the experience gained with this car, a mini-production line was prepared for the other seven, beginning with car 86 which departed at the end of 1990. The program ended with car 88 late in the summer of 1992.

Despite their age, Innsbruck's trams are maintained in pristine condition by the undertakings workshops, as exemplified in this view of car 85 at Mutters in September 1995. Built in 1961 by Düwag as 6-axle Hagen car 65, it was bought by the IVB in 1976, fitted with a former Bielefeld centre section in 1983, and then transferred to the Stubaitalbahn.   (author)

IVB No.	Type	Built	In IVB service	ex-SBV C-section	ex-HSB No.
81	8xGelZR	1961	xx.11.84	805	69
82**	8xGelZR	1968	xx.04.98	815	41
83	8xGelZR	1960	03.01.77	814	63
84	8xGelZR	1960	24.07.81	813	64
85	8xGelZR	1961	21.05.80	810	65
86	8xGelZR	1961	13.12.76	811	66
87	8xGelZR	1961	13.12.76	812	67
88	8xGelZR	1961	29.11.76	802	68
89*	8xGelZR	1961	10.04.79	805	69

* Car 89 renumbered 81 in 1984.

** Car 82 fitted with A/B sections from Bochum car 41 in 1998.

After the collision at Mutters in April 1995, the damaged A section from car 87 was replaced by the A section from car 82 to form a new number 87. The B section from car 82 and the A section from car 87 were scrapped, and the C section from car 82 placed in store pending the purchase of a replacement car.

This occurred on 29 February 1996 when GT6 car 41 arrived from Bochum. Built by Düwag in 1968, and to the same design as the Hagen cars, it was fitted with the C section from car 82 and it entered service as new car 82 in April 1998. No conductor's desks were installed, the space being utilised for the carriage of bicycles; a modification that was progressively made to the rest of the batch.

Following a scheduled overhaul, car 81 was the first of the batch to be repainted white, being returned to service in May 1998.

Trolleybuses

Type GE150M18P: 801-16

The Town Council authorised the re-introduction of trolleybuses on routes O and R in 1985. To operate these services, sixteen 3-axle articulated trolleybuses were ordered from ÖAF/Gräf & Stift, a wholly owned subsidiary of MAN of Nürnberg, at a cost of ATS 90 million (£250,000 per vehicle), with electrical equipment supplied by ASEA/BBC. Numbered 801-16, they were based on a MAN design, and painted in Innsbruck's standard red and cream livery. A single 160-kW motor provides power to the centre axle, and seated accommodation is provided for 49 passengers with space for a further 93 standing, in a body which is 18 metres long.

A small auxiliary diesel engine fitted in the rear section provides drive to the rear axle, to enable them to be moved short distances without connection to an overhead power supply. Trolleybuses entering Wilten

Typifying the first batch of trolleybuses on the current system is number 803 which is seen departing Marktplatz on a route O service to Olympisches Dorf, 09-99. (author)

depot from Pastorstrasse, during the first few years of trolleybus operation, had to resort to using this engine as there was no wiring into the depot. Electrically operated retrievers and automatic rewiring equipment was used to simplify the raising and lowering of trolley poles.

Numbers 813-6 were fitted with spraying equipment on their trolley heads, and were scheduled on the last service runs on cold and frosty evenings to apply a coat of de-icing fluid to the wires, thus preventing problems on early morning duties.

The complete batch entered service with the opening of the new system on 17 December 1988, and trolleybus 815 was the first of the series to be repainted white in May 1998.

Type NGE152M: 817-26

For the extension of the trolleybus system across the town to Allerheiligen and Peerhofsiedlung, ten more trolleybuses were ordered from ÖAF/Gräf & Stift in 1990. These were based on the MAN NG272 bus design, with low-floor front entrances and an advanced processor controlled power system from Kiepe-Elektrik. As the trolley poles no longer needed to be lowered for access to the depot they were not fitted with retrievers; a bamboo pole being carried in a tube under the rear body section in case of dewirement.

These new vehicles were numbered 817-26, and the first was displayed at the IAA Commercial Vehicle Show at Hannover in May 1992, sporting the new IVB bus and trolleybus livery of all-over white with red, black and grey bands. The complete batch was delivered during the second half of 1992, and they were put to work on the extended route O on 30 November, trolley 817 having been used on familiarisation training since 5 October.

IVB No.	Type	Design	Built	In IVB service
801-16	GE150M18P	3xGel	1988	17.12.88
817	NGE152M17	3xGel NfM	1992	05.10.92
817-26	NGE152M17	3xGel NfM	1992	04.11.92

Works cars

A small fleet of purpose-built and converted passenger cars is used for the maintenance and repair of the permanent way and overhead power supply.

Hall bogie cars 2 and 3 provide the motive power for both works and museum services. Ex-Zürich passenger car 21 was converted to Railgrinder 21 and repainted overall yellow in 1971, while snow clearance duties are fulfilled by ex-Wien snowbroom 200. Purchased from its home city in 1925 and painted in a deep maroon livery, it operates through the town streets and on the Igls and Fulpmes lines.

In addition, a number of former LBIHiT and Stb covered and open trailers, and a handful of motor vehicles, are utilized on permanent way tasks.

No.	Type	Built	Purpose
2	4xZR	1909	Permanent way
3	4xZR	1909	Permanent way
21	2xZR	1907	Railgrinder. Converted 1971
200	2xZR	1906	Snowbroom, ex-Wien 6106, 1925
203	4xZR	1918	Rail, sleeper and ballast carrier
204	4xZR	1918	Rail, sleeper and ballast carrier
211	2xZR	1900	Tanker, weed killing
217	4xZR	1967	Ballast wagon, ex-MIBRAG, 1998
228	2xZR	1908	Snowbrush, ex- Stb 28, 1984
236	2xZR	1908	Stores wagon, ex-Stb 36, 1984
237	2xZR	1904	Tower wagon, ex-Stb, 1984

A rear view of trolleybus 823 passing through Burggraben on route O. Fitted with low-floor front entrances and a little wider than the first batch, these vehicles were fitted with double rear wheels, however, trolley retrievers were omitted, 09-95. (author)

One of four motor cars donated to the IVB by the Zürich undertaking in 1954, car 21 ran in passenger service until 1971 when it was converted to a railgrinder. Painted in a mustard yellow colour it replaced railgrinder car 53 and was subsequently repainted in this cream livery with red and white stripes. Still in service, the car was photographed turning from Egger-Lienz-Strasse while participating in the centenary parade, 07-09-91. (collection Mackinger)

12. Preserved cars

The number of tramcars preserved in Innsbruck has steadily increased over the years to an extent that they currently outnumber the operational fleet. Most are owned by the TMB, and many have been restored to their original condition and liveries, but the IVB maintains a number of vintage cars for special duties, private hire and track maintenance.

The Tiroler MuseumsBahnen (TMB)

With the withdrawal of the ac cars from the Stubaitalbahn in 1983, a group of local enthusiasts set about preserving a representative selection of rolling stock and formed the Tiroler MuseumsBahnen (TMB). Two years later the entire fleet, the former depot and the Stubaitalbahnhof were handed over to the new society. Its mission was later expanded to include the collection of artefacts from tramways and light railways throughout the North and South Tirol (now part of Austria and Italy respectively).

Stb motor cars 1/2/4 and trailer 14 currently reside in the depot, awaiting the possibility of being run using power supplied from a rotary converter mounted on one of the goods wagons. Of the remaining Stb trailers all were found new homes on working railways; cars 12-13 with Eurotram at Klagenfurt and 11/17 at the Museum Bahn in Bregenzerwald where they were renumbered 101 and 103 respectively. Car 15 went to the Museum Bahn St Florian and 16 to the steam-powered rack railway at Achensee, but both were subsequently transferred to the Museum Bahn Bregenzerwald where they were renumbered 104 and 102 respectively.

Several IVB trams were gradually transferred to the museum including a five-car set comprising former Hall bogie car 4 and ex-Igls 2-axle trailer cars 101/4/5/11 in 1986. More recently other cars have returned to Innsbruck after long sojourns in tramway museums in Graz and Klagenfurt and these include; IVB 2-axle motor car 53 and the sole Breda-built bogie car 60. IVB 2-axle motor car 54 and the unnumbered snowbroom were retrieved from the Innsbruck Zeughaus in 1998.

Goods wagons 22/32 are the only former Stb cars in operational condition. Hall bogie car 4 was stripped to its frames several years ago in preparation for its restoration to 1909 condition; motor cars 53 and 54 and trailer car 142 await restoration. Eight cars have been fully restored to operational condition and are used on special occasions.

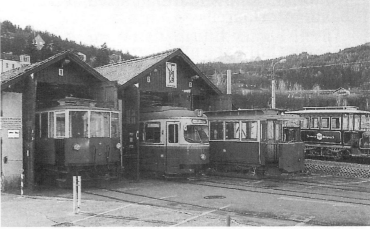

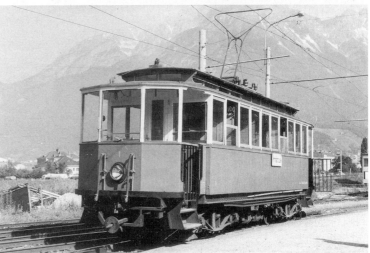

Just some of the trams in the TMB collection: (top) Stb motor car 4, IVB bogie car 61, IVB trailer car 143 and IMB trailer car 105 at the former Stubaitalbahn depot, (TMB). Stb motor car 1 seen (centre, upper) in the 1960s complete with bow collector (H. Herrmann). A rare summer outing for the unnumbered snowbroom (centre, lower) at Berg Isel in the 1950s. The bow collector was used to supply power to the motors driving the brushes only, as the car was in effect a trailer that had to be pushed around the system by a motor car. (E.Schmidt/VEF). Looking rather forlorn after its long sojourn in Graz, motor car 53 (bottom) stands outside the museum depot, 09-95. (author)

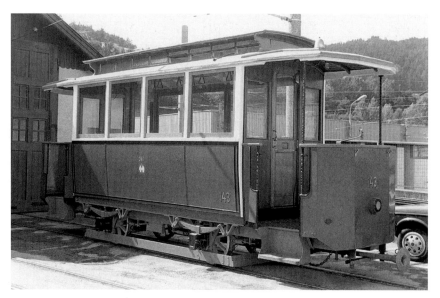

Known affectionately as the "Mailander", bogie car 60 (above left) ran in a red and silver livery for its first decade of service in Innsbruck. Here it passes a 2-axle tram set in Pastorstrasse in the early 'fifties (E.Schmidt/VEF). Bogie car 61 (above, right) provides an interesting comparison with car 60 as it turns into Brunecker Strasse with "Sonderfahrt" (excursion) in the destination display (collection Mackinger). Taken a week before the centenary parade, this view of trailer car 143 outside the museum depot (left) shows the recently applied repaint to good effect, 01-09-91. *(author)*

Trailer cars 16 and 105 were completely rebuilt to original condition and painted green between 1986-91, while car 111 was rebuilt and repainted in 1936 styling in 1995. The full set was completed in 1998 when the IVB finished work on car 104 which retains its final 1970-style livery. They form an impressive rake of historic vehicles and are often seen on tourist specials behind Hall bogie cars 2 and 3.

The museum is open on Saturdays from May to September from 09:00 to 17:00. For a modest charge,

visitors can look around an excellent display of photographs and equipment, purchase items from the book shop and inspect preserved cars in the depot.

The TMB maintains a close relationship with the Innsbrucker Verkehrsbetriebe and many restoration tasks are undertaken using the tramway undertaking's equipment and facilities.

The TMB can be contacted at: Pater-Reinisch-Weg 4, A-6020 Innsbruck or via email from its internet website; http://members.aon.at/tmb.

The current TMB fleet comprises:

Ex-Stubaitalbahn - ac					
Class	No.	Built	Builder	Type	Notes
Tw	1	1904	Graz	4xZR	Passenger motor car
Tw	2	1904	Graz	4xZR	Passenger motor car
Tw	4	1905	Graz	4xZR	Passenger motor car. Adapted for use as TMB library
Bw	14	1904	Graz/IVB	2xZR	Passenger trailer. New body 1965
Bw	16	1904	Graz/IVB	2xZR	Passenger trailer. New body 1963*
Gw	22	1904	Graz	2xZR	Open wagon, 2-axle. Restored to as delivered condition
Gw	32	1904	Graz	2xZR	Covered wagon, 2-axle. Restored to as delivered condition
Gw	34	1905	Graz	3xZR	Covered wagon, 3-axle. MB St Florian 1982, TMB 1989
* Currently on long-term loan to the Bregenzerwaldbahn. The new bodies on cars 14/6 were built in the IVB workshops.					

Ex-Lokalbahn Innsbruck Hall in Tirol & IVB

Class	No.	Built	Builder	Type	Notes
Tw	4	1909	Graz	4xZR	Passenger motor car. TMB 1986. Under restoration to 1909 condition.
Tw	19	1907	Schlieren	2xZR	Passenger motor car. Restored to 1955 condition, 1985-7
Tw	53	1909	Graz	2xZR	Passenger motor car. TM Graz 1973, TMB 1990. Awaiting restoration.
Tw	54	1905	Graz	2xZR	Passenger motor car. Zeughaus 1972, TMB 1998. Awaiting restoration
Tw	60	1942	Breda	4xZR	Passenger motor car. Eurotram 1978, TMB 1990. Restored to 1960 cond'n
Tw	61	1960	Lohner	4xZR	Passenger motor car. TMB 1989. Under restoration
Bw	16	1892	Graz	2xZR	Passenger trailer. TMB 1986. Restored to 1892 condition, 1989/90. ex-101
Bw	142	1906	Graz	2xZR	Passenger trailer. BRD 1977, TMB 1989. Awaiting restoration
Bw	143	1906	Graz	2xZR	Passenger trailer. TM Graz 1973, TMB 1990. Restored to 1970 condition
Bw	147	1907	Graz	2xZR	Passenger trailer. Restored to 1955 condition, 1985-7
Sk		1909	Graz	2xZR	Snowbroom. Zeughaus 1973, TMB 1998.

Ex-Innsbrucker Mittelgebirgsbahn & IVB

Class	No.	Built	Builder	Type	Notes
Bw	104	1900	Graz	2xZR	Passenger trailer. TMB 1986. Restored to 1970 condition, 1998/9
Bw	105	1900	Graz	2xZR	Passenger trailer. TMB 1986. Restored to 1900 condition, 1991
Bw	111	1900	Graz	2xZR	Passenger trailer. TMB 1986. Restored to late 1936 condition, 1996
Gw	262	1900	Graz	2xZR	Towerwagon. Converted from covered wagon in 1936
Gw	263	1904	Graz	2xZR	Covered wagon. TM Graz 1973, TMB 1990

Museum Cars operated by the IVB

The IVB maintains a small fleet of vintage cars for use on museum duties. Former Hall bogie cars 2 and 3 are used over the entire system, operating the *Nostalgiefahrten* and private-hire specials, with up to four of the 2-axle trailers, 102/3/6/12, or a selection of TMB trailers in tow.

In addition, Zürich 2-axle motor car 19 and Merano trailer 147 are retained as museum cars. Car 19 also operates a free public service on behalf of the TMB from Hauptbahnhof to the Stubaitalbahnhof museum at 10:25 and 14:25 on Saturdays when the museum is open.

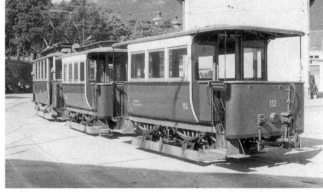

Trailer car 112 was badly damaged by the bombing in World War 2 and fitted with a brand new body in 1945; a three-window saloon replacing the original four bay design. Following withdrawal from service on the Igls line in 1981, it was assigned to the IVB museum fleet. In this 1970s scene it is being moved from the Klostergasse car sheds to the depot yard. (collection Mackinger)

Formerly Zürich number 147, 2-axle motor car 19 was withdrawn from passenger service in 1978 to become a museum car. Restored by TMB members in the mid-'eighties it is used on special occasions and for the collection of visitors to the museum from Hauptbahnhof. Here it waits to depart from Bergisel for the station, 09-95. (author)

"Mother duck and her ducklings" is the popular local term describing a Hall bogie with a rake of trailers. Here, five of the IVB's six museum cars headed by motor car 3, cross open meadows as they approach Raitis on a "Nostalgiefahrt" service to Fulpmes, 08-93. (author)

The current IVB museum car fleet comprises:

Class	No.	Built	Builder	Type	Notes
Tw	2	1909	Graz	4xZR	Passenger motor car. Works, *Nostalgiefahrten* and private hire
Tw	3	1909	Graz	4xZR	Passenger motor car. Works, *Nostalgiefahrten* and private hire
Bw	102	1900	Graz	2xZR	Passenger trailer. *Nostalgiefahrten* and private hire
Bw	103	1900	Graz	2xZR	Passenger trailer. *Nostalgiefahrten* and private hire
Bw	106	1900	Graz	2xZR	Passenger trailer. *Nostalgiefahrten* and private hire
Bw	112	1900	Graz	2xZR	Passenger trailer. *Nostalgiefahrten* and private hire

The Hungerburgbahn

Nestling beneath the Hafelekar peak (2269 m) on the north side of the city, is the Hungerburg plateau and the village of the same name. At nearly 300 metres above Innsbruck, various means of linking Hungerburg with the city were investigated at the turn of the century, including a narrow-gauge railway and cable-car line, but the steep incline excluded most forms of conventional transport. The decision was taken to build a cable-hauled funicular railway and Ing. Riehl was contracted to build the line, which would be operated by the LBIHiT. It was opened with great ceremony on 12 September 1906, with operation by two passenger cars joined by a cable at their upper ends. Drive was provided by a 180-kW motor located at the top station (858 m).

Although built for use by local inhabitants, the line soon gained importance as a tourist attraction following construction of the Nordkettenbahn cable-car line from Hungerburg to the Seegrube peak (1905 m) in 1929, and a middle station to serve Europe's highest Alpine Zoo which opened in 1987. The line climbs 287 m within its length of 840 m, on a maximum gradient of 49%. Over the years, the IVB has purchased four series of cars so as to maintain a safe and modern image, the current vehicles being built in 1982 by Bombardier-Rotax and each able to carry 92 passengers.

The Hungerburg funicular railway has provided an important link between the village high on the northern plateau and the city since 1906. (left) The two cars cross at the mid-point loop shortly after the line opened (W.Kreutz) and (lower), a car from the third series crosses the river Inn on the trestle-style bridge on the approach to the lower station, 30-08-58.   (E.W.H. Leifter)

13. Depots

Over the years several buildings were constructed to house the tram and trolleybus fleets. A small overnight car shed was in use at Hall from 1895 until 1974 and a wooden single-road car shed at Igls until the end of trailer operation in 1981. A purpose-built trolleybus depot, built at Arzl in 1952, closed with the trolleybus system in 1976. On the Stubaitalbahn, a wooden car shed erected at Fulpmes in 1904 was replaced with a more modern structure in 1983 and this continues in regular use, accommodating two Hagen cars overnight for the early morning duties.

Betriebshof Bergisel

To provide workshop and storage facilities for the rolling stock operated by the LBIHiT on the steam-powered Hall *lokalbahn*, a depot was built at Bergisel on the southern outskirts of Innsbruck, in 1891. The opening of the IMB line in 1900 and introduction of electric trams in 1905 saw a rapid expansion at this location, culminating with the erection of two wooden car sheds on the east side of Klostergasse. Also the terminus of several tram routes over the years, the depot yard had a unique atmosphere and was a fascinating place to watch the comings and goings, especially during rush-hours and other busy periods.

Built in 1951 to house the trolleybus fleet, Arzl depot (top) was a rather austere structure located in the north-east outskirts of the city. Livorno trolleybus 16 and Gräf & Stift number 25 can be seen in this 1965 view. (centre) Small sheds were erected at both Hall and Igls for holding stock overnight and that at Igls can be seen behind car 85 in this early 1980s view, (both, collection Mackinger). Berg Isel depot (below) and a scene that changed little over the years. As terminus for several routes the yard was often full with people transferring from one to another, with trams arriving and departing at both ends. Car 39 can be seen inside the shed on the left while others await attention in the former steam sheds in the background, 26-08-51. (J.Gillham)

The purchase of modern postwar cars, with their complex electrical systems and maintenance requirements, emphasised the need for more spacious and up-to-date facilities, and this became more acute with the arrival of the single-ended cars. A new depot was constructed on a large site at nearby Wilten in the late 'seventies allowing Bergisel to close on 12 October 1981. Demolition began soon after to make way for commercial offices and a terminal loop and layover tracks for routes 1 and 6. Sadly, nothing remains to indicate the former use of the site.

Betriebshof Wilten

Plans for a new depot and central workshop with full overhaul and maintenance facilities and accommodation for all IVB trams, trolleybuses and buses were published in 1972. Built on land adjacent to Stubaitalbahnhof, construction of the first phase, which comprised an administration centre and depot, began on 18 February 1974. Before it could be used for the intended purpose

however, Innsbruck was chosen as host city for the 1976 Winter Olympic Games following the withdrawal of the selected nation and, as there was no time to provide a purpose-built television, press and reception centre for the anticipated 600 people needed to staff it, the decision was taken to install these facilities in *Halle I*.

Officially opened for IVB use on 17 September 1977 and with accommodation for 40 trams and 100 buses, it was soon realised that at 10 000 m² *Halle I* would not be large enough to house the anticipated fleet of second-hand articulated cars, so a second depot, *Halle II*, was erected for the trams behind *Halle I*. With space for 56 articulated cars on 16 tracks, it would provide enough capacity to house the tramcar fleet well into the next century.

Depot accommodation for the entire fleet of trolleybuses and motorbuses, and maintenance facilities for all vehicles are provided in *Halle I*, which was later expanded with the construction of an underground storage hall.

Early morning and two Hagen cars, lead by 86 (above), are about to depart Wilten depot for Hungerburgbahn with school children brought down from the villages by the Stubaitalbahn train standing in the terminus. Following conversion to dc operation, Stb school specials were extended right through to Hungerburgbahn, 23-11-77 (W.Kreutz). A bogie car on route 1 runs slowly over temporary points known as "Kletterweiche" in Pastorstrasse, ca1976 (below), while the installation of permanent pointwork into Wilten depot proceeds. Directly behind the tram is the administration building and main workshops. (collection Mackinger)

14. Withdrawn trams and trolleybuses

Fleet No.	Built by	Renumbered No.	Date	New Role	Withdrawn Date	Notes
IVB Passenger Motor Cars						
Cars 1-8, type 4xZR, entered service 1909						
1	AEG/Graz				1974	Tramway Museum, Graz
2	AEG/Graz	1981		Works		Special duties and works
3	AEG/Graz	1981		Works		Special duties and works
4	AEG/Graz	1981		Works	1986	TMB museum car
5	AEG/Graz				1974	Eurotram, Klagenfurt
6	AEG/Graz				1981	Lokalbahn, Payerbach, then Eurotram
7	AEG/Graz				1974	Gries. Weer 1980, Eurotram 1988
8	AEG/Graz				1974	Gries. Lokalbahn Payerbach 1981, then Eurotram
Cars 13-15, type 2xZR, ex-VB Remscheid, built in 1903, entered service 1940						
13	Falkenried				1951	ex-Remscheid 13
14	Falkenried				1950	ex-Remscheid 14
15	Falkenried				1951	ex-Remscheid 15
Car 17, type 2xZR, ex-Winterthur, built in 1915, entered service 1947						
17	Winterthur				1956	ex-Winterthur 17
Cars 18-21, type 2xZR, ex-VZB Zürich, built in 1907/9, entered service 1954						
18	Schlieron/Oerlikon				1978	ex-Zürich 1146. Eurotram 1978
19	Schlieron/Oerlikon	1978		IVB Museum car		ex-Zürich 147
20	Schlieron/Oerlikon	1978		Works car		ex-Zürich 145. St Florian 1983, then Eurotram
21	Schlieron/Oerlikon	1971		Railgrinder		ex-Zürich 144
Cars 24-32, type 2xZR, ex-BVB Basel, built in 1898, entered service 1950/2/8						
24	SIG/BBC				1966	ex-Basel 37
25	SIG/BBC				1966	ex-Basel 24
26	SIG/BBC				1966	ex-Basel 26
27	SIG/BBC				1966	ex-Basel 27
28	SIG/BBC	1966		Works car	1978	ex-Basel 32. Eurotram
29	SIG/BBC				1966	ex-Basel 29
30	SIG/BBC				1966	ex-Basel 34. Cafe in Lustenau
31	SIG/BBC	1966		Works car	1978	ex-Basel 31. Eurotram
32^{II}	SIG/BBC				1966^{II}	ex-Basel 41
Cars 32-54, type 2xZR, built in 1905/8/9/11						
32	AEG/Graz				1952	
33	AEG/Graz	1954		Works car	1955	
34	AEG/Graz				1954	
35	AEG/Graz				1955	
36	AEG/Graz	1955		Works car	1959	
37	AEG/Graz				1953	body to car 48
38	AEG/Graz	1930		Railgrinder	1961	
39	AEG/Graz				1943	destroyed in bombing
40	AEG/Graz				1944	damaged in bombing, body to car 54
41	AEG/Graz				1954	body to car 51
42	AEG/Graz				1950	
43	AEG/Graz	50^{II}	1949			rebuilt as car 50^{II}
44	AEG/Graz				1960	
45	AEG/Graz				1945	destroyed in bombing
46	AEG/Graz	145	1951			rebuilt as trailer 145
47	AEG/Graz				1960	
48	AEG/Graz				1962	body from car 37 in 1953
49	AEG/Graz				1960	
50	AEG/Graz				1949	
50^{II}	AEG/Graz				1957	rebuilt from car 43
51	AEG/Graz	53^{II}	1946			rebuilt as car 53^{II}
51^{II}	AEG/Graz				1960	rebuilt from car 53
52	AEG/Graz				1962	
53	AEG/Graz	51^{II}	1950			rebuilt as car 51^{II}
53^{II}	AEG/Graz		1961	Railgrinder	1971	Tramwaymuseum Graz - TMB 1990
54	AEG/Graz				1943	destroyed in bombing
54^{II}	AEG/Graz		1960	Works car	1972	rebuilt from car 40. Zeughaus, Innsb.
Car 60, type 4xZR, built in 1942, entered service 1944						
60	Breda/Ansaldo				1977	Eurotram. TMB 1990
Cars 61-62, type 2xZR, ex-Rechtsufrige Thunerseebahn, built in 1913, entered service 1953						
61	Crede/SSW	1953		Works car	1960	ex-STJ car 6
62	Crede/SSW	1953		Works car	1961	ex-STJ car 4

IVB Passenger Motor Cars

Fleet No.	Built by	Renumbered No.	Date	New Role	Withdrawn Date	Notes
Cars 61ᴵᴵ-66, type 4xER, built in 1960						
61ᴵᴵ	Lohner/Elin		1991	Museum car	1989	TMB 1991
62ᴵᴵ	Lohner/Elin				1989	Scrapped 1989
63	Lohner/Elin				1989	Scrapped 1992
64	Lohner/Elin		1993	Museum car	1989	Eurotram 1993
65	Lohner/Elin				1989	Scrapped 1992
66	Lohner/Elin				1989	Scrapped 1993

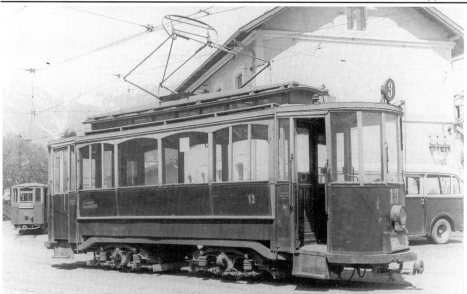

The end saloon windows on the Remscheid cars received body-bracing towards the end of their working lives as can be seen on car 13 (above) at Berg Isel, ca1950. There are also signs of platform droop (collection Mackinger). Looking very smart after recent overhauls, motor car 48 and trailer 147 await their scheduled departure time at the Rudolf-Greinz-Strasse terminus of route 3 in May 1950 (right). Three years later, the body on car 48 was scrapped and replaced with that from car 37. (below) Also looking smart was former STJ car 61, photographed at Berg Isel before entering service on route 4 in 1953. It was, however, unable to run to schedule and was transferred to works duties with sister car 62.　　　　　(both, W.Kreutz)

IVB Passenger Trailer Cars

Fleet No.	Built by	Renumbered Old No.	Date	New Role	Withdrawn Date	Notes
Cars 101-141, type 2xZR, built in 1891/2/3/1900						
101	AEG/Graz				1945	destroyed in bombing
101^{II}	IVB	122	1947	TMB Museum car	1981	rebuilt from car 122, 3 windows. To TMB 1989, restored as replica of car 16, 1990
102	AEG/Graz		1981	IVB Museum car	1981	rebuilt in 1937, 2 windows
103	AEG/Graz		1986	IVB Museum car	1981	
104	AEG/Graz		1986	TMB Museum car	1981	refurbished to withdrawn condition, 1998
105	AEG/Graz		1986	TMB museum car	1981	rebuilt to original condition, 1991
106	AEG/Graz		1981	IVB Museum car	1981	rebuilt in 1937, 2 windows
107	AEG/Graz				1945	destroyed in bombing
108	AEG/Graz				1970	Cafe in Lustenau
109	AEG/Graz				1955	rebuilt as car 140^{II}
110	AEG/Graz				1954	rebuilt as car 138^{II}
111	AEG/Graz		1986	TMB Museum car	1981	rebuilt as 1930s condition
112	AEG/Graz		1981	IVB Museum car	1981	damaged in bombing, new body 1945
113	AEG/Graz	1	1911		1950	rebuilt as open car in 1930
114	AEG/Graz	2	1911		1950	rebuilt as open car in 1931
115	AEG/Graz	3	1911		1966	rebuilt in 1939, 2 windows
116	AEG/Graz	4	1911		1970	Cafe in Lustenau, then Eurotram
117	AEG/Graz	5	1911		1977	rebuilt in 1947, clerestory removed. Eurotram
118	AEG/Graz	6	1911		1967	rebuilt in 1937, 2 windows
119	AEG/Graz	7	1911		1975	rebuilt in 1938, 2 windows. Gries in 1975, Schmalzerhof, Weer in 1980, then Eurotram
120	AEG/Graz	8	1911		1974	rebuilt in 1938, 2 windows. Dr. Daimer (Gräf & Stift) in 1974
121	AEG/Graz	9	1911		1975	rebuilt in 1937, 2 windows. Gries in1975, Schmalzerhof, Weer in 1980, then Eurotram
122	AEG/Graz	10	1911		1947	rebuilt as car 101^{II}
122^{II}	AEG/Graz	137	1950		1975	rebuilt in 1950 from car 137, flat roof. Gries in 1975, Schmalzerhof, Weer in 1980, then Eurotram
123	AEG/Graz	11	1911		1975	rebuilt in 1937, 2 windows. Eurotram.
124	AEG/Graz	12	1911		1974	Zeughaus Innsbruck
125	AEG/Graz	13	1911		1958	
126	AEG/Graz	14	1911		1970	Second-hand car dealer, Jünger
127	AEG/Graz	15	1911		1944	destroyed in bombing. Summer car rebuilt with doors and windows, 1941
128	AEG/Graz	16	1911		1948	Summer car rebuilt with doors and windows, 1941
129	AEG/Graz	17	1911		1974	rebuilt with doors and windows in 1959. Museumstram St Polten, then Eurotram
130	AEG/Graz	18	1911		1957	Summer car rebuilt with doors and windows, 1941 Body transferred to car 140^{II}
131	AEG/Graz	19	1911		1950	Summer car rebuilt with doors and windows, 1941
132	AEG/Graz	20	1911		1945	destroyed in bombing
133	AEG/Graz	21	1911		1954	Summer car rebuilt with doors and windows,1941 To Fa. Nussbaumer Kaffee, Gmunden
134	AEG/Graz	22	1911		1945	destroyed in bombing
135	AEG/Graz	23	1911		1974	Eurotram, Klagenfurt
136	AEG/Graz	24	1911		1962	Strassenbahn museum, Leidschandam (Holland)
137	AEG/Graz	25	1911		1950	rebuilt as car 122^{II}
138	AEG/Graz	26	1911		1954	
138^{II}	AEG/Graz	110	1954		1974	rebuilt in 1954 from car 110. Tramway Museum Graz
139	AEG/Graz	27	1911		1977	rebuilt in 1947, flat roof. Eurotram
140	AEG/Graz	28	1911		1955	damaged in storm
140^{II}	AEG/Graz	109	1955		1955	rebuilt in 1955 from car 109. Body transferred from car 130 in 1957. Private-buyer, Raitis in 1975
141	AEG/Graz	29	1911		1959	rebuilt in 1937, 2 windows
Cars 142-145^{II}/148, type 2xZR, built in 1906/52						
142	AEG/Graz		1977	TMB Museum car	1977	rebuilt after bomb damage in 1943. Private buyer in Germany. TMB in 1989
143	AEG/Graz		1973	TMB Museum car	1973	Tramwaymuseum Graz. TMB in 1990
144	AEG/Graz		1978		1978	Eurotram, Klagenfurt
145	AEG/Graz				1943	destroyed in bombing
145^{II}	IVB	46	1952		1967	rebuilt on truck from motor car 46
148	IVB				1977	New build in 1952. Eurotram, Klagenfurt

Trailer car 148, seen above at the Rudolf-Greinz-Strasse terminus with Basel motor car 28, had a comparatively short life. Built by the IVB in 1952 from leftover parts from the postwar rebuilding program, it was withdrawn in 1977 and moved to the Eurotram line in Klagenfurt. *(collection Mackinger)*

Bringing up the rear of this route 1 three-car set, headed by motor car 51 and trailer 109, is trailer 130. One of four 1892-built, open-sided summer cars, it was brought out of storage in 1941 and fitted with a fully-enclosed saloon. In 1957, its body was transferred to trailer 140 after that car was badly damaged in a storm. The location is Berg Isel in the early 1950s. *(E.Schmidt/VEF)*

Cars 146/7, type 2xZR, ex-Strassenbahn Lana-Meran in 1917, built in 1907, entered service 1917

| 146 | AEG/Graz | 53 | 1917 | | 1978 | ex-Merano 53. Rebuilt in 1947 and 1956. Eurotram, Klagenfurt in 1980 |
| 147 | AEG/Graz | 54 | 1917 | IVB Museum car | 1978 | ex-Merano 54. Rebuilt in 1947 and 1956. IVB Weihnachtsbahn |

Cars 151-160, type 2xZR, ex-BVB Basel in 1950/2, built in 1908, entered service 1950/2

151	BVB	282	1950		1966	ex-Basel 282
152	BVB	284	1950		1966	ex-Basel 284
153	BVB	286	1950		1961	ex-Basel 286
154	BVB	287	1950		1965	ex-Basel 287
155	BVB	288	1950		1966	ex-Basel 288
156	BVB	289	1950		1966	ex-Basel 289
157	BVB	293	1950		1965	ex-Basel 293
158	BVB	290	1952		1966	ex-Basel 290
159	BVB	291	1952		1966	ex-Basel 291
160	BVB	292	1952		1966	ex-Basel 292. Eurotram in 1977

Cars 161/2, type 2xZR, ex-Rechtsufrige Thunerseebahn, built in 1913, entered service 1953

| 161 | Crede | 52 | 1953 | | 1954 | ex-STJ 52. To Stb in 1954 |
| 162 | Crede | 32 | 1953 | | 1954 | ex-STJ 32. To Stb in 1954 |

IVB Goods Wagons

Goods wagons, type 2xZR, 3xZR, built 1891-1918

201	Graz				1964	2-axle open trailer, built 1891
202	Graz				1961	2-axle open trailer, built 1891
212	Graz				1961	2-axle open trailer, built 1900
251	Graz				1961	2-axle covered trailer, built 1891
252	Graz				1950	2-axle covered trailer, built 1891
253	Graz		1973	museum car	1973	2-axle covered trailer, built 1893
261	Graz				1950	2-axle covered trailer, built 1900
263	Graz		1973	museum car	1973	2-axle covered trailer, built 1904
264	Graz				1959	2-axle brine trailer, built 1895

Sparkling in the sunshine outside the Klostergasse sheds are Basel trailer car 160 (right) and STJ trailers 162 and 161 (left). Following withdrawal in 1966, car 160 was sold to a camp site and moved on to Eurotram in 1977. The TMB hope to oversee its return to Innsbruck one day. The former Thun cars were transferred to the Stubaitalbahn in 1954 and scrapped in 1967.

(both, collection Mackinger)

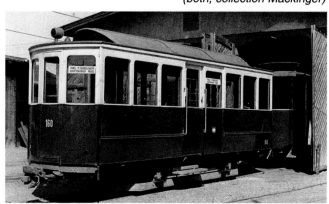

Stb - Passenger Motor Cars

Fleet No.	Built by	Renumbered Old No. Date		New Role	Withdrawn Date	Notes
Cars 1-4, type 4xZR, built in 1904/5						
1	AEG/Graz			TMB museum car	1983	TMB in 1985
2	AEG/Graz			TMB museum car	1983	TMB in 1985
3	AEG/Graz				1982	
4	AEG/Graz			TMB museum car	1983	TMB in 1985

Stb - Passenger Trailer Cars

Fleet No.	Built by	Renumbered Old No. Date		New Role	Withdrawn Date	Notes
Cars 11-17, type 2xZR, built in 1904/63-7						
11	AEG/Graz				1983	Museumsbahn, Bregenzerwald in 1986
12	AEG/Graz				1983	Eurotram, Klagenfurt in 1985
13	AEG/Graz				1983	Eurotram, Klagenfurt in 1985
14	AEG/Graz			TMB museum car	1983	TMB in 1985
15	AEG/Graz				1983	Museumsbahn, St Florian in 1985
16	AEG/Graz				1983	Achenseebahn in 1985
17	IVB				1983	Achenseebahn in 1985. Museumsbahn, Bregenzerwald in 1988
Cars 161/2, type 2xZR, ex-Rechtsufrige Thunerseebahn, built in 1913, entered service 1954						
161	Crede	52	1953		1967	ex-STJ 52. ex-IVB 161
162	Crede	32	1953		1967	ex-STJ 32. ex-IVB 162

Stb Goods Wagons

Fleet No.	Built by	Renumbered Old No. Date		New Role	Withdrawn Date	Notes
21	Graz				1980	2-axle open trailer, built 1904
22	Graz					2-axle open trailer, built 1904
23	Graz				1971	3-axle open trailer, built 1905
24	Graz		1984	snow clearing		3-axle open trailer, built 1905
25	Graz				1982	2-axle open trailer, built 1907
26	Graz				1971	2-axle open trailer, built 1907
27	Graz				1971	3-axle open trailer, built 1908
28	Graz		1984	snow clearing		3-axle open trailer, built 1908
29	Graz				1980	3-axle open trailer, built 1912
30	Graz				1982	3-axle open trailer, built 1912
31	Graz				1963	2-axle covered trailer, built 1904
32	Graz		1982	museum car	1982	2-axle covered trailer, built 1904
33	Graz		1980	museum car	1980	3-axle covered trailer, built 1905
34	Graz		1982	museum car	1982	3-axle covered trailer, built 1905
35	Graz		1982	museum car	1982	2-axle covered trailer, built 1907

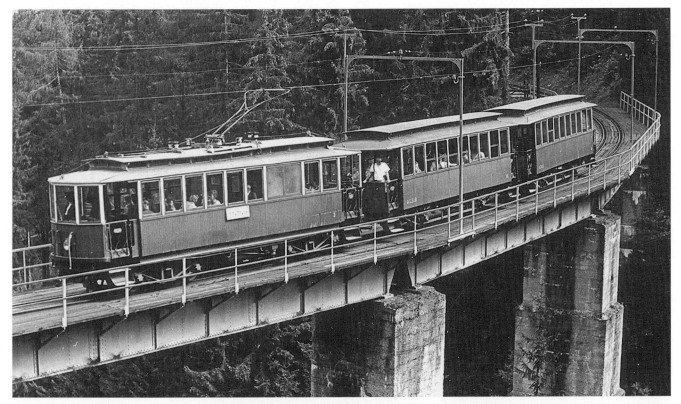

After more than fifty years service on the Stubaitalbahn, the ac stock still looked very much as it did when built. Here, ill-fated motor car 3 hauls trailers 16 and 11 across the Mutterer Brücke en-route for Innsbruck, 03-10-58. (A. Luft)

IVB Trolleybuses

Trolleybuses 10-14, ex-VB Roma (from batch numbered 4001-15), built in 1936, entered service 1944

10	Breda/TIBB			1951	Scrapped 1956
11	Breda/TIBB			1951	Scrapped 1956
12	Breda/TIBB			1946	Scrapped 1955
13	Breda/TIBB			1954	Scrapped 1956
14	Breda/TIBB				Scrapped 1955. Used for spares only

Trolleybuses 15-18, ex-VB Livorno (from batch numbered 1-35), built in 1935/6, entered service 1944/53

15	Fiat/CGE			1972	Scrapped 1976
16	Fiat/CGE			1972	Became rest room for construction Co.
17	Fiat/CGE			1972	Scrapped 1976
18	Fiat/CGE			1972	Scrapped 1976. Spares source, 1944-53

Trolleybuses 19-22, ex-VB San Remo (ex-2-4/7), built in 1941, entered service 1944

19	Fiat/CGE	1971	museum vehicle	1971	DSM, Hannover
20	Fiat/CGE			1971	Mentlberg Zoo
21	Fiat/CGE	1971	museum vehicle	1971	Eurotram
22	Fiat/CGE			1971	Became rest room for construction Co.

Trolleybuses 23-28, built in 1948/9, entered service 1948/9, rebuilt by Gräf & Stift in 1963/4

23	Gräf & Stift/BBC			1976	Became rest room for construction Co.
24	Gräf & Stift/BBC			1976	Electrical equipment to Eurotram
25	Gräf & Stift/BBC			1976	Became rest room for construction Co.
26	Gräf & Stift/BBC	1976	museum vehicle	1976	DSM, Hannover
27	Gräf & Stift/BBC	1976	museum vehicle	1976	Eurotram
28	Gräf & Stift/BBC			1976	Became rest room for construction Co.

Trolleybus trailers 221/3/4, built in 1943, entered service as bus trailers in 1943

221	Lohner			1970	Adapted for trolleybus use in 1951
223	Lohner			1970	Adapted for trolleybus use in 1951
224	Lohner			1970	Adapted for trolleybus use in 1953

Looking in need of attention, former Roma trolleybus 13 stands outside the newly-built Arzl depot in a shabby red and silver livery in August 1951. It ran in service until 1954 and was scrapped two years later.
(H. Wöber)

By contrast, former San Remo trolleybus 22 looks in pristine condition as it waits on the Arzl terminal loop prior to taking up duties on route B, 26-08-59. On withdrawal in 1971, it was sold for use as a rest room to a construction company. *(collection Mackinger)*

Technical specifications

IVB motor cars

Fleet Nos.	Builder	Year Built	Length metres	Weight tonnes	Seats	Capacity	Motors kW	Type	Notes
1-8	AEG/Graz	1909	11.95	18.50	30	60	2x36.8	4xZR	a,b,c
13-15	Falkenreid	1903	9.40	10.60	22	47	2x35	2xZR	d
17	Winterthur	1915	8.57	10.50	16	44	2x25.7	2xZR	e
18-21	Schlieren	1907/9	8.20	12.80	18	42	2x54	2xZR	f
24-32^{II}	SIG/BBC	1898	8.71	11.70	16	43	2x39	2xZR	g
32-54	AEG/Graz	1905/11	7.80	9.10	16	32	2x21.7	2xZR	
60	Breda	1942	13.70	16.50	26	116	4x33	4xZR	h
61/62	Credé/SSW	1913	9.00	12.00	18	34	2x33	2xZR	i
61^{II}-66	Lohner/Elin	1960	13.40	14.90	25	76	2x100	4xZR	
71-77	Lohner/Elin	1966	19.40	21.70	40	112	2x100	6xGelER	
31^{II}/33^{II}-42^{II}	DÜWAG	1957/63	19.30	19.30	35	113	2x100	6xGelER	j
51^{III}-53^{II}	DÜWAG	1963/66	25.80	24.40	56	153	2x100	8xGelER	j,k
81-88	DÜWAG	1960/61	26.71	27.30	59	152	2x110	8xGelZR	l,m

IVB trailer cars

Fleet Nos.	Builder	Year Built	Length metres	Weight tonnes	Seats	Capacity	Motors kW	Type	Notes
101-141	AEG/Graz	1891/1900	5.85	3.20	16	38		2xZR	n
142-145^{II}	AEG/Graz	1906/52	7.53	4.80	16	44		2xZR	o
146/147	AEG/Graz	1907	8.58	6.00	12	54		2xZR	p
148	IVB	1952	7.53	4.80	16	44		2xZR	q
151-160	BVB	1908	8.08	5.50	20	55		2xZR	g
161	Credé	1913	8.54	6.60	24	36		2xZR	i,r
162	Credé	1913	8.60	7.10	24	36		2xZR	i,r

Stb motor cars

Fleet Nos.	Builder	Year Built	Length metres	Weight tonnes	Seats	Capacity	Motors kW	Type	Notes
1-3	AEG/Graz	1904	11.40	20.50	38	66	2x30	4xZR	
4	AEG/Graz	1905	11.90	21.00	36	62	2x30	4xZR	

Stb trailer cars

Fleet Nos.	Builder	Year Built	Length metres	Weight tonnes	Seats	Capacity	Motors kW	Type	Notes
11-16	AEG/Graz	1904/63-6	10.00	7.0	36	63		2xZR	s
17	IVB	1967	10.00	7.0	36	63		2xZR	
161	Credé	1913	8.54	6.60	24	36		2xZR	i,r
162	Credé	1913	8.60	7.10	24	36		2xZR	i,r

Trolleybuses

Fleet Nos.	Builder	Year Built	Length metres	Weight tonnes	Seats	Capacity	Motors kW	Type	Notes
10-14	Breda/TIBB	1936	10.00		22	59	1x99		t
15-18	Fiat/CGE	1935/6	10.00		21	61	2x28.5		u
19-22	Fiat/CGE	1941	10.00		22	51	2x55.8		v
23-28	Gräf/BBC	1948/9	10.00		24	63	1x85		
801-16	ÖAF/Gräf & Stift/ABB	1988	18.00		49	142	1x160	3xGel	
817-26	ÖAF/Gräf & Stift/Kiepe	1992	17.50		47	142	2x149	3xGel NfM	

Notes:

a	4/7/8 fitted with 4x36.8-kW motors in 1932/40/1 respectively.
b	2/3 fitted with 4x68-kW motors in 1940/36 respectively.
c	1/5 fitted with 2x61.5-kW motors in 1941.
d	Commandeered from Remscheid, Germany in 1940.
e	Donated by the town of Winterthur, Switzerland in 1947 - transferred to the IVB in 1948.
f	Donated by the city of Zürich, Switzerland in 1954.
g	Bought second-hand from Basel, Switzerland in 1950/2.
h	Bought from the Italian manufacturer Breda in 1944.
i	Bought second-hand from the STJ, Thun, Switzerland in 1953
j	Bought second-hand from Bielefeld, Germany in 1980/2/3.
k	53^{II} converted from 6-axle car 32^{III} in 1991.
l	Bought second-hand from Hagen, Germany in 1976. Converted to 8-axle between 1980-5.
m	82^{II} fitted with A and B sections from Bochum car 41 in 1998.
n	113-41 ex-LBIHiT cars 1-29.
o	New body built for car 145^{II} by IVB in 1951/2 on truck salvaged from motor car 46.
p	Bought second-hand from Merano, South Tirol in 1917. Rebuilt in IVB workshops in 1947.
q	New car built by the IVB in 1952 to the same design as cars 142-5.
r	Transferred to the Stb in 1954.
s	New bodies built on original trucks in IVB workshops between 1963-6.
t	Commandeered from Rome, Italy in 1943 - 14 used as source of spares and never entered service.
u	Commandeered from Livorno, Italy in 1943 - 18 used as source of spares until 1953 before entering IVB service.
v	Commandeered from San Remo, Italy in 1944.

The Kreithererbrücke is one of two bridges that carry the Stubaitalbahn across deep ravines and it's trestle-style supports are clearly visible in this view as car 86 heads north towards Innsbruck during the first winter of dc operation on the line, 06-03-84. — *(G.Breitfuss)*

(BACK COVER) (upper) Trolleybuses returned to the streets of Innsbruck in 1988 and the system has steadily expanded in the intervening period. Trolleybus 825 was delivered in 1992 painted in a white livery which is gradually being applied to the rest of the IVB fleet, and was photographed operating a route O service at the Marktplatz interchange in September 1999.   *(author)*

(lower) Services on route 6 to Igls are operated by cars purchased from Bielefeld between 1980 and 1983. In support of a drive to promote greater use of the line, car 53 was painted in this striking colour scheme in 1997 and provision made in the rear for the carriage of bicycles. It is seen here passing Wilten Basilica en-route to Hauptbahnhof in September 1997.   *(author)*

Light Rail Transit Association

The LRTA is a UK-based international organisation campaigning for the construction, retention and development of modern tramways and light rail. Membership is open to everyone; all members receive the monthly magazine

Tramways & Urban Transit

by post.

Membership details from

The Membership Secretary,
LRTA,
23 Shrublands Close
Chigwell Essex IG7 5EA

Annual Subscriptions normally run to the end of the calendar year, with different rates for the UK, mainland Europe and outside Europe.

Full details are obtainable from the address above

There is also a quarterly (mainly UK) historical magazine

Tramway Review;
available to members at a reduced subscription.
Ask for details.

Information can also be found on our website

www.lrta.org

LRTA PUBLICATIONS

This book was published by LRTA PUBLICATIONS.

If you liked it, you will find that we publish (sometimes jointly) books on international tramways (some available currently and others in preparation include national handbooks on Germany, the former Soviet Union, Portugal, Switzerland and Austria).

We also publish a series of regional handbooks of British tramways, and a limited number of hardback histories, mainly of the the London area.

Recent additions include
West Midlands and East Scotland

LRTA members often have the opportunity to buy newly published LRTA books (and sometimes others) at discounted prices.

Send for booklist from:

LRTA Publications
13A The Precinct, Broxbourne, Herts EN10 7HY

or see our website

www.lrta.org

other titles by this author include:

Freiburg: From classic tramway to light rail (1998)

GREAT SAXOPHONE SOLOS

Easy Jazz Singles Russell Stokes

Seiko chromatic tuner lights

Exclusive Distributors:
Music Sales Limited
14-15 Berners Street, London W1T 3LJ, UK.

Music Sales Pty Limited
120 Rothschild Avenue, Rosebery, NSW 2018, Australia.

Order No. AM989846
ISBN 13: 978-1-84772-002-3
This book © Copyright 2007 by Wise Publications.

Unauthorised reproduction of any part of this publication by
any means including photocopying is an infringement of copyright.

Compiled and edited by Heather Slater.

Printed in the EU.

Your Guarantee of Quality:
As publishers, we strive to produce every book to the highest
commercial standards. This book has been carefully designed to minimise
awkward page turns and to make playing from it a real pleasure.
Particular care has been given to specifying acid-free, neutral-sized paper made
from pulps which have not been elemental chlorine bleached. This pulp is from farmed
sustainable forests and was produced with special regard for the environment.
Throughout, the printing and binding have been planned to ensure a sturdy,
attractive publication which should give years of enjoyment.
If your copy fails to meet our high standards, please inform us and we will gladly replace it.

www.musicsales.com

This publication is not authorised for sale
in the United States of America and/or Canada.

Wise Publications
part of The Music Sales Group
London/New York/Paris/Sydney/Copenhagen/Berlin/Madrid/Tokyo

FILM THEMES

POPULAR HITS

JAZZ & BLUES